WHEN THE WALL CAME DOWN

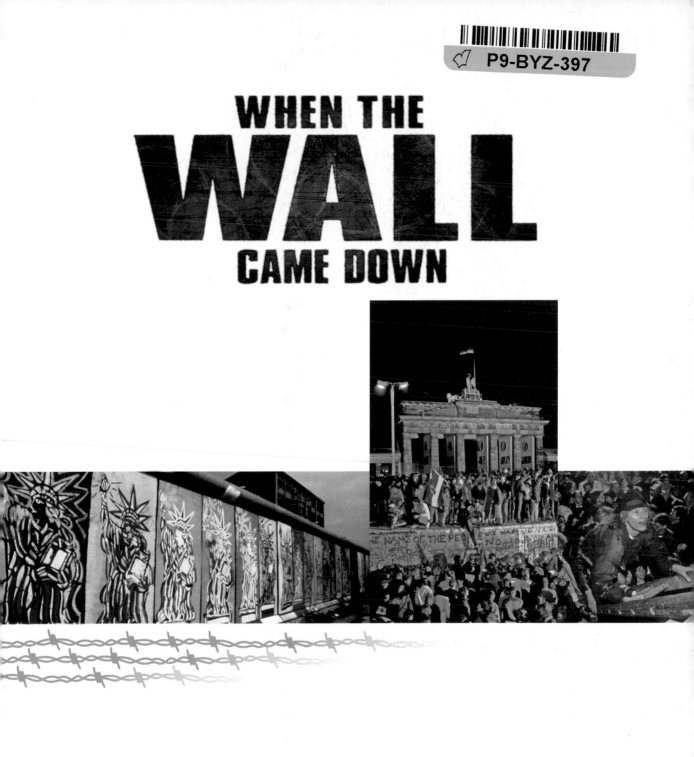

A **New York Times** BOOK

WHEN THE WALL CAME DOWN

THE BERLIN WALL
AND THE FALL OF
SOVIET COMMUNISM

SERGE SCHMEMANN

KINGFISHER
BOSTON

KINGFISHER

a Houghton Mifflin Company imprint
222 Berkeley Street
Boston, Massachusetts 02116
www.houghtonmifflinbooks.com

First published in hardcover in 2006
First published in paperback in 2007
2 4 6 8 10 9 7 5 3 1
1TR/0807/PROSP/PICA(PICA)/128MA/C

The type for this book was set in Adobe Garamond.
Book design by Anthony Cutting
Additional design by Carol Ann Davis
Edited by Deirdre Langeland
Cover design by Mike Buckley
Photo research by Maggie Berkvist

LIBRARY OF CONGRESS CATALOGING-IN-PUBLICATION DATA
Schmemann, Serge, 1945–
When the wall came down: the Berlin Wall and the fall of Soviet Communism/by Serge Schmemann.—1st ed.
p. cm.
Includes bibliographical references and index.
1. Berlin Wall, Berlin, Germany, 1961–1989—History. 2. Germany (East—Politics and government. 3.
Communism—Europe, Eastern—History—20th century. 4. Germany—History—Unification, 1990. I.
Title.
DD881.S269 2006
943'.1087--dc22
2005023892
ISBN 978-0-7534-6153-2
Printed in China

To my children, Anya, Sasha, and Natasha,
who witnessed these great moments.

A note on the articles:
Articles from the archives of *The New York Times* appear
throughout this book. These articles have been edited to fit the
format of the book. Please refer to the original article for full text.

A Note to the Reader

History is often best told by the people who witnessed it. In 1989, when the Berlin Wall came down, Serge Schmemann was chief *New York Times* correspondent in Germany. The wall, which divided the German capital, was a powerful symbol of the cold war, and its fall evoked strong reactions on both sides. Serge moved among the crowds as Berliners danced, wept, and celebrated one of the great moments in German history. Later that year, he traveled through Eastern Europe as one Communist government after another toppled under the will of its people.

74

This book tells the story of those monumental events from Serge's perspective. Throughout his story, you'll see symbols (left) that include a page number. Follow those symbols to the back of the book to read stories from the archives of *The New York Times* that provide more detail and background to pivotal events in the text.

Contents

In 1989, the city of Berlin was completely surrounded by Communist East Germany.

ONE
A Knock on the Door

November 9, 1989. A chilly evening in West Berlin. I was in my hotel room, writing furiously on my laptop. The stories were breaking fast. The Communist government in East Germany was in crisis. All through the autumn, East Germans had been fleeing their country in droves through Hungary and Czechoslovakia. Even greater numbers had been holding regular marches in East German cities, demanding reform. The government's authority was crumbling. Every day there were new changes, new announcements, new surprises.

I had just returned from a press conference in East Berlin, at which the Communist leaders had announced new travel regulations for East Germans who wanted to visit the West. That was big news: up to then, the majority of East Germans, like most Eastern Europeans, had been prevented from leaving the East. It was a good story, probably page one, so when somebody knocked on the door around midnight, I was annoyed. It was my assistant from East Berlin, Victor Homola.

"I'm busy, Victor," I barked. "Grab something from the minibar and wait."

"But, Serge..."

"Not now! Not now..."

Then it struck me: Victor? He was an East German! He wasn't allowed to cross into the West; he'd never even *been* to the West.

"Victor! What on earth are you doing here?"

"That's what I'm trying to tell you, Serge! The wall is down!"

That began one of the most exciting stories I've covered as a foreign correspondent: the fall of the Berlin Wall. For many, the event has come to represent the end of forty years in which Eastern Europe was held captive by the Soviet Union. But it was not only a political story. It was also an intensely human story, about people rising up to break down a wall that had kept them brutally apart—a wall that had divided Germany, and all of Europe, into a free and democratic West and an East that lived under dictatorship. It was about people choosing freedom.

I grabbed my West German assistant, Tom Seibert, and with Victor we jumped into a taxi. The streets near the Berlin Wall were quickly filling with celebrating Germans, and the police were trying to divert traffic. The taxi driver, a big woman with a bigger voice, was yelling out the window, *"Ich habe hier drei Pressefritzen!"*—

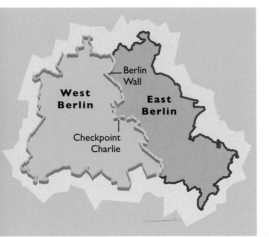

The Berlin Wall enclosed West Berlin, dividing it from East Berlin and East Germany.

"I have three press guys here!"—and the police waved us through. We drove right up to the most important stretch of the wall—the spot where it passed by the Brandenburg Gate, once the very center of Berlin.

The Berlin Wall was a frightening sight, a twelve-foot-high concrete barrier that divided one of the major cities of Europe right in half. It did more than that—since West Berlin was deep inside East Germany, the wall actually ran all around it, creating a large urban island of the free, democratic, and brightly lit West right inside the tightly controlled Communist-ruled East. The worlds inside and outside the wall were completely different—within its wall, West Berlin looked like any large Western city. Shiny Mercedes and BMW sedans cruised the neon-lit Kudamm—the grand Kurfürstendamm boulevard; store windows displayed the latest in fashions; restaurants and nightclubs were open late into the night. West Berlin had theaters, museums, a university, skyscrapers, two airports, a lake, rivers, canals, parks, even a zoo. West Berliners could easily

Diners at a sidewalk café on the Kurfürstendamm, West Berlin's lively shopping boulevard.

go to West Germany, or anywhere else in Western Europe, so they felt free and secure inside their walled-in island.

On the East German side of the wall, large blocks of anonymous apartment buildings loomed. There were far fewer shops, and everything seemed grayer and poorer. The East Germans heated their buildings with poor-quality coal, so everything was covered with soot. Still, parts of East Berlin had retained the old-fashioned charm of a central European city, recalling old black-and-white spy movies.

This view from the west side of the wall shows typical blocks of apartment buildings in East Berlin.

The Brandenburg Gate was surrounded by a no man's land enclosed by the Berlin Wall (right) and police barriers to the east (left).

In fact, life in East Berlin was better than in Moscow and many other Eastern European cities. But the East Germans were always aware of the bright lights in the Western island in their midst. West Germany deliberately aimed radio and television signals eastward, so it was easy for most East Germans to receive them. East German teenagers were more savvy about what was happening in the West than teenagers in other parts of Eastern Europe—and because of that they were much more frustrated. Though it was West Berlin that was encircled, many East German children grew up thinking the wall was around *them.*

The wall itself reflected the difference between the two governments it divided—from the Eastern side, it was like a prison wall, with watchtowers and glaring lights; from the West, or from inside, it was covered with bright and ever-changing graffiti.

Before Berlin was divided, the Brandenburg Gate had been the city's most famous landmark. Now, the gate was actually part of the Berlin Wall. The main wall ran past it on the west side, while police barriers on the east formed a no man's land around it. For decades, trying to cross that no man's land had meant possible death or imprisonment for East Germans.

Now, joyful East Berliners were scaling the barriers and running to the wall. On our side, West Germans were climbing up on top of the wall and reaching down to haul up their Eastern cousins. An observation platform on the Western side, built so visitors could look at the Brandenburg Gate, was full of dancing people.

"The wall is gone! The wall is gone!" people chanted. As we watched,

76

more and more East Germans poured over, and more and more West Germans gathered to greet them with tears and champagne. For thirty years, these people had dreamed of the day when they could be together again. Tom, a university student from Bonn who was my interpreter and assistant in West Germany, was seized by the excitement and started climbing up the wall to join the party.

I grabbed him by the foot and yelled, "Not tonight! Tonight we work. Tomorrow we celebrate!" And work we did. It was close to five a.m. when we finished filing the stories. The historic front page of the next day's *New York Times* had my story with a picture across the whole page of people dancing in front of the Brandenburg Gate. Over it, the huge headline read: "EAST GERMANY OPENS FRONTIER TO THE WEST FOR EMIGRATION OR VISITS; THOUSANDS CROSS."

In the popular German tabloid *B.Z.*, a headline screamed, *"Die Mauer ist Weg! Berlin ist wieder Berlin!"*—"The Wall Is Gone! Berlin Is Again Berlin!"

78

East and West Berliners celebrate on the Berlin Wall on November 10, 1989.

(Inset) The front page of the November 10, 1989, issue of *The New York Times* was filled with stories about the opening of the wall.

TWO
Burdened by History

Why was the opening of the Berlin Wall greeted with such emotion by the Germans? It was, after all, a national border, at least from the East German point of view, and borders all around the world are hard to cross.

But this was no simple border. The wall represented the division of Europe as a result of one of the most horrible wars ever fought, World War II. Symbolically, it divided not only a city but an entire nation, an entire continent. The division was painful for all of Europe, but for the Germans it was a special agony. They had started the war and they had been defeated at an incalculable loss in lives and property. The division of Germany had been carried out by the countries that had conquered them. Half of their own country was off-limits to them. Part of Germany lived under an authoritarian dictatorship while the other half prospered in a free democracy, and there was nothing they could do about it. Years went by, a new generation grew up, but still the Germans were always reminded by the Berlin Wall that they were not yet welcome back into the family of normal nations, that their crimes were not forgotten, that they were not forgiven.

The Germans have a long history as a culture and as a people, but for most of it they have been divided into small principalities and states. A unified German state came into being only in 1871, hundreds of years later than France and Great Britain and almost a hundred years after the Americans formed the United States. Yet in its first century, Germany was involved in two massive wars and had committed the worst genocide in history. The rise of Germany was one of the triggers for the First World

Europe at the start of World War II. Half of Czechoslovakia was "under the protection" of Germany, and Austria had been fully annexed.

ATLANTIC
OCEAN

*Norwegian
Sea*

*North
Sea*

SWEDEN

FINLAND

NORWAY

ESTONIA

*Baltic
Sea*

LATVIA

DENMARK

LITHUANIA

DANZIG

EAST
PRUSSIA

SOVIET
UNION

IRELAND

UNITED
KINGDOM

THE
NETHERLANDS

Berlin

BELGIUM

GERMANY

POLAND

LUXEMBOURG

CZECHOSLOVAKIA

CARPATHIAN
RUTHENIA

FRANCE

SWITZERLAND

AUSTRIA

HUNGARY

ROMANIA

YUGOSLAVIA

PORTUGAL

SPAIN

ITALY

BULGARIA

ALBANIA

GREECE

Mediterranean Sea

Hitler Youth celebrate National Socialist Party Day at a rally in Nuremburg in 1933.

War, which lasted from 1914 to 1918. That war totally changed the map of Europe, ending the rule of many old imperial dynasties, such as the Hapsburgs in Austria, the Hohenzollerns in Germany, the Romanovs in Russia, and the Ottoman rulers in Turkey.

But the end of World War I did not resolve all the issues that had caused it. Germany was defeated, and the victors imposed severe penalties on the losers, leaving the German economy a shambles. Many people were left without jobs, and the German currency rapidly lost value. It dropped so fast, in fact, that as soon as people got paid they would run to the stores to buy something before the money lost any more value. Prices often doubled within a few hours. By the end of 1923, a loaf of bread cost 200 billion marks, and an American dollar was worth more than one trillion marks. Paper money was so worthless that housewives started burning it in their stoves because it was cheaper than using it to buy fuel. The Germans were left feeling humiliated and resentful.

The conditions were ripe for a ruthless leader, and soon an Austrian soldier named Adolf Hitler rose to power by exploiting the grievances of the German people with an angry ideology of racial hatred and militarism. The Germans were not a defeated nation, he declared. They were actually the "master race" of "Aryans," a supposedly pure race destined to rule the world. The Aryans needed "living space" to fulfill their destiny, which was to create a great empire, the Third Reich (the Holy Roman Empire was the first, and the German Empire that fell in World War I was the second).

Hitler and his National Socialist party (the Nazis) first tried to seize power by force. They failed, and Hitler spent nine months in prison. But he returned to rebuild the Nazis into a powerful party that won elections to the Reichstag, the German parliament. In 1933, Hitler took charge of the German government, and soon he established himself as the dictatorial leader of Germany—the führer. He rebuilt the German army into the strongest in Europe and set off to conquer an empire.

Using the threat of his newly restored military, Hitler was able to quickly expand the borders of Germany without firing a shot. In 1936, he reclaimed the Rhineland, an area along the western border of Germany that had been demilitarized at the end of World War I. Then he turned his attention to Germany's eastern borders. Faced with the might of the German army, and a lack of support from other nations, Austria was annexed by Germany in 1938, and by March 1939, all of Czechoslovakia had become a part of the Reich.

The first military conquest was Poland, which the Germans invaded on September 1, 1939. The German army perfected a tactic called *blitzkrieg*—lightning war—which called for fast-moving tank attacks on several fronts at the same time. Before the attack, the Germans had reached a secret agreement with the Soviet Union to divide Poland between them, and while the Germans attacked from the west, the Soviets invaded from the east. By the start of October, Poland was totally conquered. Although Great Britain declared war on Germany, neither Great Britain nor France, the major powers in Europe, was able to send troops to defend the besieged country.

In April 1940 the Germans suddenly attacked Denmark and Norway, and a month later they marched through The Netherlands and Belgium into France.

Printed in 1923, the 500 million mark note signaled the worst of the German inflation that followed World War I.

Survivors of the Buchenwald concentration camp were liberated by Allied forces in April 1945.

(Center) Adolf Hitler with Nazi officials in Paris, July 15, 1940, one month after the German army marched into France.

Nobody could resist them. The British army, which had crossed into continental Europe to try to stop the Nazi advance, retreated across the English Channel. By the end of 1940, Hitler controlled most of continental Europe and had begun a bombing campaign against England. In 1941 he was moving against Yugoslavia and Greece. Then in June 1941, Hitler violated the German treaty with the Soviet Union and launched a massive surprise attack on his former ally. Hitler seemed unstoppable.

At the same time, the Nazis began ridding Germany and other lands they had conquered of various classes of people they regarded as "undesirable"—above all the Jews, but also Slavs (mainly Russians and Poles), Gypsies, Communists, the mentally and physically disabled, homosexuals, and political dissidents. As the persecution grew more and more intense, the Nazis began to talk of a "final solution of the Jewish question"— a horrendous plan to kill all European Jews. By the end of the war, 6 million Jews had been killed in special death camps, a genocide that we now know as the Holocaust. At least 5 million people of non-Jewish descent were also murdered.

The invasion of the Soviet Union turned out to be the turning point in Hitler's fortunes. First the invasion became bogged down by the bitter Russian winter. Then the Germans suffered a massive military defeat in the Battle of Stalingrad. The city (now called Volgograd), an industrial center on the Volga River in southwestern Russia, was a major German objective, and the German armies besieged it in August 1942.

The Dome of St. Paul's Cathedral shows through the smoke during a German air raid on London, December 29, 1940.

But the Russians did not give up, and after many months of amazingly brutal warfare, the Soviet Red Army turned the battle around, trapping and destroying the German forces in and around Stalingrad. The battle for Stalingrad was the bloodiest in history. Both sides fought without regard to cost, and between 1 and 3 million soldiers and civilians died. Nothing was left of the city. But the battle changed the course of the war. The Germans and their allies, the Axis powers, never recovered from the loss of equipment, soldiers, and morale, and before long the Red Army was driving them back.

On June 6, 1944, D-Day, the United States, Great Britain, Canada, and France launched a huge offensive from the west, landing on the Normandy beaches in northern France in the biggest seaborne invasion in history. Germany was now being squeezed from two sides, by the Soviet Union from the east and the United States and its allies from the west. In December 1944, the German army made a final effort to attack the Western Allies and to capture the important port of Antwerp. But the U.S. Third Army, under General George Patton, blocked the Germans in what came to be known as the Battle of the Bulge. By then, the Red Army was at the prewar borders of Germany.

In February 1945, the leaders of the United States, Great Britain, and the Soviet Union met in Yalta, on the Black Sea. The three unlikely allies, President Franklin D. Roosevelt, Prime Minister Winston Churchill, and Soviet leader Joseph Stalin, made plans for a coordinated attack on Germany and agreed on the division of the country once it was defeated. The treaty, known as the Yalta Agreement, would have a profound impact on the lives of Germans in the decades to come.

In the spring of 1945, the Soviet army reached Berlin, and on April 30, 1945, with his special underground bunker surrounded by Russian troops, Adolf Hitler killed himself. Germany surrendered a few days later, on May 7. Much of Europe, and most of Germany, was in ruins. Seventy percent of the city of Berlin had been destroyed. World War II had also been fought in Asia, where the United States and its allies had battled Japan, and where the Americans had introduced the atomic bomb. All told, close to 60 million people were killed. No war had ever been so terrible or so costly.

The leaders of the Allied countries meet at Yalta, February 9, 1945. From left to right: Winston Churchill (England), Franklin Roosevelt (U.S.), and Joseph Stalin (Soviet Union).

THREE
From World War to Cold War

But the world was not at peace. Even before the war ended in Europe, a new confrontation was taking shape between the United States and the Soviet Union. Though they had been allies against Germany, they represented rival ideas and saw each other as potential enemies. Joseph Stalin, the Soviet dictator, had already taken advantage of the war to seize control of the Baltic states of Lithuania, Latvia, and Estonia, and there was no doubt that he wanted to spread the Soviet system to Eastern Europe.

The Yalta Agreement left the Soviet Union free to extend its control to the Eastern European countries that the Red Army occupied, from Poland in the north to Romania in the south. That's just what Stalin did, fixing elections and assassinating anyone who opposed politicians who were loyal to the Soviet government in Moscow.

Many Eastern Europeans have called this the "Western betrayal," saying that for all their talk about

At the annual May Day parade, Soviet troops march through Moscow's Red Square in front of a poster of the fathers of Soviet Communism, Lenin, Engels, and Marx.

freedom and democracy, the Western Allies did nothing to keep the Soviet Union from grabbing their countries and in doing so condemning them to forty years under Soviet dictatorship. But at the time the agreement was made, the Allies were in no shape to start another major war against the Soviet Union. The United States was still fighting against Japan in Asia, and Britain and France still had colonies to police. Still, Yalta remains a dark blot in Western history. On May 7, 2005, President George W. Bush made a speech in Latvia in which he described the Yalta deal as "an attempt to sacrifice freedom for the sake of stability."

The author (left), with colleagues from the Moscow bureau of *The New York Times*, crosses Red Square in front of St. Basil's Cathedral in 1983.

As for Germany, the Allies agreed to disarm the country and break it up into four zones of occupation—American, Soviet, British, and French. Parts of eastern Germany were given to Poland and the Soviet Union, and their 15 million inhabitants were expelled. The capital, Berlin, was also to be divided into four occupation zones.

And so with the end of one great war, another one got under way—this one a "cold war," without actual combat but with fierce and often dangerous competition. With the defeat of Germany and Japan, and with much of Europe and Asia in ruins, two countries stood as superpowers, with military and industrial might far greater than that of any other country or groups of countries: the United States and the Soviet Union.

They represented two completely different systems. The United States had a democratic political system, under which people could elect their representatives and enjoyed broad individual freedoms. They could speak, worship, and travel freely, and they were free to start private businesses.

82

In the Soviet Union, the Communist Party had come to power in the Russian Revolution in 1917, teaching that all property should be held communally and that privately owned businesses or property should be abolished. In reality, Stalin turned the Soviet Union into a giant police state. He ordered mass purges in which thousands of people were executed on false charges. He set up a system of forced-labor camps, known as the Gulag, to which millions of people were sent to work, and to die, in appalling conditions. Stalin's successors shut down the camps after his death in 1953, but the Soviet people continued to live in fear of the state and its secretpolice until the state finally collapsed in December 1991.

I first arrived to work in Moscow as a correspondent for *The New York Times* in 1980, so I caught the last years of the old Soviet Union. We Westerners who worked there lived in guarded compounds where it was very difficult for ordinary Russians to visit us. Every time I went out, even to walk my dog, I was followed by the secret police, the KGB. Our phones were tapped, and we never knew whether we could trust the Russians we met. Western newspapers and books were largely forbidden. All the newspapers and the radio and television stations were run by the state, and giant jamming towers sent out loud noise signals to block radio transmissions from the West. People who challenged the system, tried to leave, or tried to practice their religion were arrested or harassed. Very few people were allowed to travel to the West.

Under the terms of the Yalta Agreement, Germany was divided into four zones of occupation. The three Allied sectors were later combined.

A sign posted at a military checkpoint marked the boundary between the American and Soviet sectors in 1960.

After Stalin imposed his system on Eastern Europe, many people in the West feared that he would try to spread Communism to other countries—particularly developing countries, where widespread poverty often made the idea of communally held property popular. President Dwight D. Eisenhower compared the threat of Communism spreading to a row of dominoes falling. If one country toppled, he believed, the rest would soon fall. This became known as the domino theory.

Strong Communist parties arose in many Western countries. In the United States, fear of the Communists led one senator, Joseph McCarthy of Wisconsin, to launch a massive witch-hunt, in which many people's lives and careers were ruined because they were suspected of belonging to subversive organizations.

Nowhere were the Communist and non-Communist systems as close to each other as in Berlin, where the Soviets and the Western Allies controlled adjacent zones. So almost immediately after World War II came to an end, Berlin became like a dangerous fuse in the East-West confrontation, the place where the cold war could suddenly turn hot.

The city of Berlin was entirely within the eastern part of Germany, which was occupied by the Soviet army. But the Allies had decided to also divide Berlin into occupation zones. Accordingly, the shattered German capital was divided into four zones—American, Soviet, British, and French. The Soviets, whose own industry had been almost completely destroyed in the war, quickly stripped their zone of whatever factories, machinery, and other equipment they could transport back to Russia. The Western Allies, by contrast, merged their zones into what came to be known as West Berlin and began to introduce Western economic and political practices.

In effect, the Western zone created a democratic enclave in the middle of Soviet territory, and Stalin did not like that. So he decided to drive the Allies out. At six a.m. on June 24, 1948, the Red Army suddenly threw a blockade around West Berlin, cutting off all roads and rail lines.

In effect, the Soviets intended to starve the city into submission, much as a medieval army might try to besiege a fortress until those inside collapsed from hunger and exhaustion.

That posed a difficult dilemma for the Western Allies. They were not willing or ready to start a new war, this time with the Soviet Union, which had far stronger forces in Europe than they did. But if the Western powers abandoned Berlin, they feared that the Russians might be tempted to seize other countries and perhaps the rest of Germany.

So the United States came up with an audacious plan. It would try to supply West Berlin with everything it needed—food, fuel, clothes, *everything*—by air. Fortunately, the United States Air Force had a general who had done it before, William H. Tunner. In World War II, General Tunner had led an operation to keep American forces in China supplied by air from India, which meant flying over the Himalaya Mountains. When he arrived in Berlin, things didn't look very promising. "My first overall impression was that the situation was just as I had anticipated— a real cowboy operation. Few people knew what they would be doing the next day," he said.

Children in West Berlin cheer at an American plane bringing supplies into the city past the Soviet blockade in 1948.

**The Soviet
Union** and its
sphere of control.
Countries in pink
were republics of
the Soviet Union.
Countries in purple
were considered
Soviet satellites.

But Tunner did it. He eventually had a C54 "Skymaster," a propeller-driven cargo plane capable of carrying ten tons, landing or taking off from West Berlin's two airports every thirty seconds, day and night. They brought in an average of 8,000 tons of supplies a day. Most of this was food and coal, but it also included cargo like food for the animals in the Berlin zoo, chocolate for Christmas, paper for the newspapers, seedlings to replace trees that had been cut down, even Volkswagen cars for the Berlin police. The planes usually returned to the West empty, but sometimes they carried goods that had been manufactured in West Berlin, which proudly bore the stamp "Made in blockaded Berlin." The constant drone of the airplanes over the besieged city became the sound of freedom to its residents.

Finally, on May 12, 1949, the Soviet Union lifted the siege. When the first trucks arrived by land, huge crowds gathered to greet them. The airlift continued for another four months, to build up reserves in case the Soviets tried another siege. But the West had passed its first great test, and no more territory would fall to the Soviet Union.

But a new struggle had begun. There was no longer one Germany occupied by its conquerors but two Germanys separately occupied by East and West. A few days after the blockade was lifted, the American, British, and French occupation zones were formally combined into one country, the Federal Republic of Germany, or West Germany. Three months later, the United States, Canada, and most of the non-Communist countries in Europe joined to form an alliance, the North Atlantic Treaty Organization (NATO), in which they pledged to support each other if any of them was attacked.

The Soviet Union was not far behind. On September 23, 1949, U.S. president Harry S. Truman announced that the Soviet Union had exploded its own atomic bomb, matching a doomsday weapon that until then only the United States had possessed. Two weeks later, the Soviets created the German Democratic Republic, or East Germany, in their

84

occupation zone. And in 1955, Moscow formed its own alliance—the Warsaw Pact—with its seven Eastern European satellite states.

Europe was now formally divided into two enemy camps—the Western NATO camp, led by the United States, which included West Germany, Britain, France, Italy, and other Western European countries; and the Eastern Warsaw Pact camp, led by the Soviet Union, which included the countries the Soviet Union controlled after the war—East Germany, Poland, Czechoslovakia, Hungary, Romania, Albania, and Bulgaria.

The Soviet Union ruled its satellites with an iron hand. Any rebellion was ruthlessly crushed. In June 1953, a labor strike by East German workers turned into a mass uprising. Soviet tanks rolled in, leaving many dead. In 1956, the Soviet army invaded Hungary to put down a rebellion, and in 1968 it crushed another in Czechoslovakia.

Both the United States and the Soviet Union developed vast arsenals of nuclear weapons, which could soar over continents and oceans in a matter of minutes. The power of these weapons was beyond imagination: combined, they were capable of destroying the entire earth. The arms race did not stop even there: both powers launched massive space programs to spy on each other.

The confrontation was not limited to Europe. In Asia, Communists under Mao Tse-tung seized control over most of China. A war over Korea ended up with the partition of the

A crowd in Budapest gathers around a statue of Joseph Stalin, toppled by demonstrators during the Hungarian revolt of 1956.

(Below middle) Protestors in East Berlin throw stones at a Soviet tank during the uprising of 1953, which began as a simple labor protest.

country into a Communist North Korea and a U.S.-backed South Korea, a divide that remains to this day. In Vietnam, a war between the Communist north and the non-Communist south eventually led the United States to intervene. More than 500,000 American soldiers fought in Vietnam.

The war was very unpopular in the United States, and eventually the Americans withdrew, allowing a North Vietnamese victory. In 1962, an attempt by the Soviet Union to base nuclear missiles in Cuba, where they would be within easy firing range of the United States, brought the world to the brink of World War III. The cold war also spread to underdeveloped countries of the Third World, which were constantly pressured to make a choice between the United States and the Soviet Union and often fell victim to manipulation by the superpowers.

In a famous speech in March 1946, a year after World War II ended, the great British wartime leader Winston Churchill had introduced the term "iron curtain" for the line that divided East and West. "From Stettin in the Baltic to Trieste in the Adriatic, an iron curtain has descended across the continent," he said in a famous speech. "Behind that line lie all the capitals of the ancient states of central and Eastern Europe. Warsaw,

Berlin, Prague, Vienna, Budapest, Belgrade, Bucharest, and Sofia; all these famous cities and the populations around them lie in what I must call the Soviet sphere, and all are subject, in one form or another, not only to Soviet influence but to a very high and in some cases increasing measure of control from Moscow."

That iron curtain ran right through the heart of Europe, of Germany, and of Berlin.

Students in Prague heckle Soviet soldiers who were sent to restore Communist leadership in Czechoslovakia in August 1968.

FOUR

Suddenly, a Wall Goes Up

The East Germans got the raw end of the division of their country. As in other Eastern European countries, they were forced by the Soviet Union to adopt a Soviet-style Communist dictatorship. The ruling party—which in East Germany was called the Socialist Unity Party of Germany (SED)—controlled every aspect of life, from the media to religion. It kept all information in its grip, making sure that nothing critical of the state or of its leaders was ever published or broadcast. It even controlled the courts and the labor unions. The Ministry of State Security, the feared secret police known as the Stasi, maintained a huge network of 90,000 secret police and 175,000 paid informants watching what people said and did. In a population of 17 million, that worked out to one spy for every sixty-four people. They kept files on 4 million East Germans—a quarter of the population.

The East German people learned early on that as long as the Soviet Union stood behind their government, resistance was futile. The Soviet crackdown during the 1953 labor strike had made that clear.

Still, through hard work, the East Germans succeeded in rebuilding much of their country and in building up one of the strongest economies in the Soviet Bloc, especially in machine building, chemicals, and energy. In fact, East German industrial production ranked fifth in Europe and eighth in the world. The standard of living was far higher than in Soviet Russia, and better than in many other Eastern European countries.

Far larger than East Germany, West Germany emerged from the ruins of World War II to build the most prosperous country in Europe and the third-largest economy in the world (after the United States and Japan). This "economic miracle" created global respect for German machinery and automobiles—such as Mercedes, BMW, Volkswagen. The West Germans enjoyed a thriving democracy; they were one of the founders of the European Community, which eventually became the European Union, and a charter member of NATO. The West Germans lived well, with good pay, good social benefits, and the freedom to travel the world over.

That wide difference in standards of living created a major headache for the Soviet and East German leaders, and it was the reason the wall went up. Though a barrier was built between East and West Germany soon after the two countries were formally established, there were no barriers separating East and West Berlin all through the 1950s, so people could get from the Soviet-controlled East to the free West as easily as crossing the street.

And cross they did. The more oppressive East Germany became, the more East Germans fled west. Walter Ulbricht, the head of the East German Communist Party, repeatedly asked the Soviet leader Nikita Khrushchev to get the Western Allies out of West Berlin. But Khrushchev, who had succeeded Stalin in 1953, was trying to change from confrontation to a "peaceful coexistence" with the West, and he resisted any action that could create new tensions. By the 1960s, the situation was dire for East Germany. The East German economy was in danger of collapse as professionals and workers left in droves, and the numbers kept rising. In 1960, almost 200,000 escaped, including 688 doctors, 296 dentists, and 2,648 engineers. In 1961, the rate doubled— by midsummer 207,000 were gone. By mid-August, a full fifth of the East German population had fled.

Khrushchev had no choice. On August 13, 1961, Berliners woke up to find coils of barbed wire and armed guards down the middle of the

The Brandenburg Gate on November 6, 1961, after Allied authorities put up barbed wire in response to the barrier being built by East Germany.

city. Many friends and even families were divided, some for many years, some forever. It was an amazing admission of failure by the Communists; in effect, they acknowledged that the only way they could keep people in their part of the world was by force. Years later, Ulbricht admitted that the wall was his greatest propaganda defeat, a glaring symbol of the failure of the Communist system. But he insisted that he had no alternative: East Germany had been bleeding to death.

86

Before the wall's completion, many people escaped. Here, an East German soldier leaps over the barbed wire into West Berlin on August 15, 1961.

In the first weeks after the barrier went up, it was still possible for people to get across, either by jumping over the barbed wire or by leaping from houses that were right on the border. West Berliners would spread a net out under a building and several East Berliners would quickly jump out a window. Many people tried tunneling under the barrier. One tunnel led out of a graveyard—people would pretend to be mourning and then would drop out of sight. Some people flew over the wall. To avoid suspicion, one group bought small amounts of nylon cloth until they had enough to make a hot-air balloon.

But escape was extremely dangerous. East German border guards had orders to shoot. On August 24, 1961, Günter Litwin became the first person to be shot and killed trying to cross the wall. That same week, a woman died leaping from a fourth-floor window, and a twenty-four-year-old man was shot swimming across a canal. In all, more than 5,000 people tried to escape over the wall, and more than 250 died. Bernd Lünser was shot trying to escape on a clothesline strung over the wall; Udo Düllick drowned after being shot swimming across the Spree River; Winfried Freudenberg died in the crash of his hot-air balloon. One of the best-known victims was Peter Fechter, eighteen, who was shot while trying to climb over the wall on August 17, 1962, exactly a year after it went up. He was left to bleed to death in full view of the West.

The Berlin Wall was not finished overnight. At first it was coils of barbed wire. Then the East Germans raised a cement barrier. Then this was replaced with more sophisticated panels of reinforced concrete, each twelve feet high and topped by smooth round pipes, so someone trying to clamber up could not get a grip. The completed wall stretched ninety-six miles around West Berlin, with alarms, spotlights, guard dogs, heavily armed border guards, 302 watchtowers, and 20 bunkers. There were also forty-one miles of wire mesh fencing and sixty-five miles of trenches to block vehicles. It was impossible to be in West Berlin and not be aware of the wall. It crossed streets, went around blocks, and squeezed along

88

the sides of buildings. Where it crossed a river or a canal, there were iron barriers built to the very bottom of the water in case someone tried to swim under it. In some stretches the wall came right up against buildings; in others it included a hundred-yard-wide no man's land.

The American president in 1961 was John F. Kennedy. On the August afternoon that the wall went up, he was sailing off his family's estate at Hyannis Port, Massachusetts. When the urgent bulletin came from Washington that the East Germans were setting up a barrier, a U.S. Army major rushed into the surf to get word to Kennedy's military aide. "Why in hell didn't we know about it?" Kennedy asked, not really expecting an answer. "What can we do now?" There was nothing the United States *could* do. If it tried to break the barrier by force, it could mean war.

The next summer, Kennedy visited Berlin. He rode through the city for four hours; he stood gazing a long time over the wall, and he wrote what became one of the most famous speeches of all time. Standing in front of more than a million people outside city hall on June 26, 1963, Kennedy delivered a ringing tribute to West Berlin and to the spirit of freedom.

East Germans build the first stages of the Berlin Wall in 1961.

President John F. Kennedy (far right) looks over the wall from a viewing platform during his visit to Berlin on June 26, 1963.

"There are many people in the world who really don't understand, or say they don't, what is the great issue between the free world and the Communist world," Kennedy proclaimed, chopping the air for emphasis. "Let them come to Berlin!

"There are some who say that communism is the wave of the future. Let them come to Berlin!

"And there are some who say, in Europe and elsewhere, we can work with the Communists. Let them come to Berlin!

"And there are even a few who say that it is true that communism is an evil system, but it permits us to make economic progress. *Lass' sie nach Berlin kommen!* Let them come to Berlin.

"Freedom has many difficulties and democracy is not perfect. But we have never had to put a wall up to keep our people in—to prevent them from leaving us."

Kennedy spoke of the courage of the Berliners: "I know of no town, no city, that has been besieged for eighteen years that still lives with the vitality and the force, and the hope, and the determination of the city of West Berlin." The wall, he said, was "an offense not only against history but an offense against humanity, separating families, dividing husbands and wives and brothers and sisters, and dividing a people who wish to be joined together."

He declared that through their suffering and patience the Germans had earned the right to freedom: "In eighteen years of peace and good faith, this generation of Germans has earned the right to be free, including the right to unite their families and their nation in lasting peace, with good will to all people." He looked prophetically to the future: "Let me ask you, as I close, to lift your eyes beyond the dangers of today, to the hopes of tomorrow, beyond the freedom merely of this city of Berlin, or your country of Germany, to the advance of freedom everywhere, beyond the wall to the day of peace with justice, beyond yourselves and ourselves to all mankind."

And then Kennedy concluded with a ringing declaration of solidarity that would become a rallying cry for West Berlin until the wall came down twenty-seven years later: "All free men, wherever they may live, are citizens of Berlin. And, therefore, as a free man, I take pride in the words '*Ich bin ein Berliner.*' I am a Berliner."

After that magnificent speech, it became popular for presidents and politicians to come to West Berlin to shake their fist at the wall, establishing it as the most infamous barrier in the world. It became the symbol for the oppression in Communist countries, the proof for the West that its system was better. In June 1987, twenty-four years after Kennedy spoke—and when Mikhail Gorbachev was introducing reforms to the Soviet Union—President Ronald Reagan came to West Berlin and made another speech that would be much quoted:

"General Secretary Gorbachev, if you seek peace, if you seek prosperity for the Soviet Union and Eastern Europe, if you seek liberalization: Come here to this gate! Mr. Gorbachev, open this gate! Mr. Gorbachev, tear down this wall!"

Gorbachev did. Or, at least, he stood aside when the people tore it down.

FIVE
The Revolution Spreads

I **was in Moscow when Mikhail Gorbachev came to power on March 11, 1985. The Soviet Union had been stagnating under a progression of doddering old Communist leaders who ruled through fear and inertia.** The few people who criticized the system, known as dissidents, were regularly sent to prison, and the government fought desperately to keep Western information and ideas out. But the absence of information served only to push the Soviet Union further behind the West, where widespread access to computerized information was opening a new era. More and more Communists were beginning to understand that unless the system allowed some freedom of expression and thought, it would grind to a halt. Finally the last of the old leaders died and Gorbachev was chosen as the new leader. He had just turned fifty-six, and he was impatient to reform the system from top to bottom.

Charismatic, energetic, and resolute, Gorbachev started to change things on all fronts. In speech after speech, day after day, he demanded a "decisive breakthrough" or "resolute measures." He called for a complete restructuring—perestroika—of the economy; he declared war on alcoholism, which was killing off Russian men at a worrisome rate; he cracked down on government corruption; he called for an end to the cold war with the United States, declaring that it was time to end the "ice age of their relations." And, most important, he called for more openness in society—the Russian word was *glasnost,* or "giving voice." For seventy years, it had been a crime for Russians to speak their mind, and suddenly

President Ronald Reagan (left) greets Soviet leader Mikhail Gorbachev at a summit meeting in Reykjavik, Iceland, on October 20, 1986.

they were being urged to do so. Perhaps Gorbachev was not aware of what he was setting loose; it turned out to be the start of a revolution.

Congressman Thomas P. O'Neill, Jr., the Speaker of the U.S. House of Representatives, was one of the first Western leaders to visit Moscow after Gorbachev came to power, and he was clearly taken by the new leader. "He appeared to be the type of man who would be an excellent trial lawyer, an outstanding attorney in New York had he lived there," O'Neill said. "There is no question that he is a master of words and a master in the art of politics and diplomacy."

The new approach was immediately felt throughout Soviet society. It was as if a lid had been raised on the pent-up creativity of the nation. Writers who had been hounded by the Kremlin now sang Gorbachev's praises. People flocked to him when he went into the streets, something none of the earlier Soviet leaders ever dared. On one trip to Leningrad, Gorbachev was crushed by well-wishers, including a large, buxom woman who was pressed right up against him. "Just get close to the people and we'll not let you down," she shouted. Gorbachev broke into a big smile and asked, "Can I be any closer?" The crowd loved it.

Soon, the hostilities with the West began to break down. President Ronald Reagan, who had famously called the Soviet Union an "evil empire," met with Gorbachev and was charmed. New arms-control agreements were reached, reducing the threat of a nuclear war. It was a thrilling time to be in Russia, as people began to awaken, to dream, to talk freely.

Gorbachev is surrounded by well-wishers on a visit to Prague, Czechoslovakia, in 1987.

The excitement soon spread to Moscow's Eastern European allies. Until then, relations with these countries were dictated by what was known as the Brezhnev Doctrine: If any country tried to break away from Soviet control, Moscow claimed the right to intervene by force, as it had in Berlin in 1953, in Hungary in 1956, and in Czechoslovakia in 1968. No more, Gorbachev said.

The Eastern Europeans were free to go their own way, and Moscow would not interfere. The new policy came to be jokingly called the "Sinatra Doctrine" after Gorbachev's witty spokesman, Gennady Gerasimov, told reporters, "The Brezhnev Doctrine is dead. You know the Frank Sinatra song 'My Way'? Hungary and Poland are doing it their way. We now have the Sinatra Doctrine." To show that he meant business, Gorbachev pulled Soviet troops out of Afghanistan, where they had been bogged down trying to prop up a Communist government since 1980.

But before the wave of freedom swept through Eastern Europe, it ran into a wall in China. Gorbachev made a visit to Beijing in 1989, inspiring Chinese students to demand the same reforms for their country. They began to hold regular demonstrations in the central square of Beijing, Tiananmen. The crowds rapidly expanded into the millions. But the Communist rulers did not bend; instead, they sent tanks into the square on June 4, 1989, to crush the rebellion in a brutal massacre.

But in Eastern Europe, Gorbachev's glasnost spread like a tsunami. It turned out that the Americans had been right about the domino theory. But instead of the non-Communist countries falling like dominoes to Communism, it was the Communist countries that tumbled.

In June 1989 Poland held the first free elections in postwar Eastern Europe. The Solidarity Party, which had sprung from a labor union founded earlier in the decade, won a stunning victory over the Communist Party. That was the first signal that once the Communist parties were left on their own, they stood little chance of winning real elections. The wave swept on to Hungary, and through Hungary reached East Germany.

In August 1989, Hungary announced that it would no longer keep its border with Austria sealed tight the way Communist governments had until then. In effect, the Hungarians opened a crack through the iron curtain. Since East Germans were allowed to travel to Hungary, which was part of the Soviet Bloc, they now had an exit route once again to West Germany, where they were automatically greeted as fellow German citizens. So the East Germans began to flee again, as they had before the Berlin Wall went up. The East German government tried to close the hole by barring their people from going to Hungary, so the East Germans started fleeing to other Eastern European countries, to Poland and Czechoslovakia, flooding the West German embassies within those countries and demanding to be let out. There was no way to stop them.

Lech Walesa, a founder of the Solidarity labor movement, campaigns for the first Polish election in May 1989.

I remember the excitement in October 1989 when trains packed with escaping East Germans pulled into Hof, in West Germany. More than 6,000 arrived just on that day, bleary-eyed after the ten-hour train trip. Some had spent weeks camped inside West German embassies in Warsaw or Prague. Others had come over at the last minute. One of these was Heike Schubert, a twenty-two-year-old

East German refugees, escaping across the Hungarian border into Austria, pose with their passports on September 11, 1989.

hairdresser from Halle, in East Germany, and her boyfriend, Andreas Stolz, twenty. Crying with relief and fatigue, Heike described how she and Andreas had gone to her parents to tell them they were leaving, and her parents had said, "You go on. We'd do the same if we were young and had the possibility."

94

At the same time, an even greater challenge to Communist government was growing inside East Germany. It began when small groups gathered in churches and then held candlelit vigils outside to demand more freedom. The protests rapidly grew into massive weekly marches, especially in the industrial city of Leipzig. I remember standing at the side of the street in Leipzig as wave after wave of marchers swept past in the night, many holding candles. It was a powerful testimony to the people's longing for freedom, and it seemed totally unstoppable. But the East German leader, Erich Honecker, was deaf to the protesters' demands. He was defiantly preparing huge celebrations to mark the fortieth anniversary of East Germany in October, and his security chiefs were ominously talking of the "Chinese solution." Something had to give.

Honecker was a tough old Communist. A miner's son, he had been a Communist all his life, had studied in Stalin's Moscow, and had been jailed for eight years by the Nazis. When the Soviets had installed a Communist government after World War II, Honecker quickly clambered to the top. He and the old loyalists around him were firmly opposed to the reforms Gorbachev was pushing from Moscow. After the massacre in China's Tiananmen Square, Egon Krenz, the East German security chief, had sent a message to the Chinese authorities, congratulating them. Honecker had been in charge of building the wall in 1961, and now, at seventy-seven, he still insisted that it would be standing "another fifty, one hundred years." The words *glasnost* and *perestroika* were barred from East German radio and newspapers, in Russian or German, and Soviet publications were not distributed. Honecker was not about to allow any loosening of the system; on the contrary, he wanted the fortieth anniversary to be a show of strength.

But there was no way Honecker could avoid inviting the leader of the Soviet Union to attend, and in early October, Mikhail Gorbachev arrived in East Berlin. Wherever he went, the Russian leader drew crowds of cheering pro-democracy demonstrators. On the evening of October 6, Gorbachev stood at Honecker's side for a torchlight parade of Communist youths; on the next day, October 7, Gorbachev was again at Honecker's side at a formal military parade. But it was the last hurrah of the old regime. Before he left East Berlin, Gorbachev spoke with a group of journalists: "I believe that dangers await only those who do not react to life." It was clear to Honecker that unless he started responding to the demands for more freedom, he would be cast aside.

Inspired by Gorbachev, several members of a small new opposition movement, New Forum, called for a demonstration on October 7 on East Berlin's main square, Alexanderplatz. New Forum had been formed by left-wing intellectuals who did not want to flee west and who did not want a reunification with the capitalist West. They wanted a reformed, Socialist East Germany, and Gorbachev was their hero.

(Center) As part of a ceremony marking the withdrawal of Russian troops from Hungary in May 1989, a Soviet soldier dances with a Hungarian in national costume.

But as with everything else in those days, the streets set their own pace and their own agenda. The demonstration quickly swelled into a massive protest. I remember wondering where on earth all these people were suddenly materializing from. Only the day before, thousands of docile East German Communist youths had marched through these same streets. Now thousands of pro-reform youths were chanting "Gorby! Gorby!"

The police were as surprised as I was. They stood in front of the bridge across the Spree River to block the demonstrators from the parliament and the row of embassies and official buildings along the Unter den Linden boulevard. But the police were not used to demonstrations. The crowd began to throw coins at the officers, as if to say that they had sold out to the Communist bosses. It was a defining moment: the Gorbachev revolution had come within a stone's throw of the Berlin Wall.

Blocked in one direction, the demonstrators turned toward a working-class district called Prenzlauer Berg. There, residents leaned out their windows to cheer, and the crowd grew larger. A line of young Communists with red armbands tried to block one street, but the demonstrators went right through them, chanting *"Keine Gewalt!"*— "No violence!" It was dark now, and the feeling of power and tension was growing by the minute. Finally the police waded in, battering and grabbing demonstrators at random and driving them onto side streets. I was swept back by retreating demonstrators, and before long it was all over. More than a thousand protesters had been arrested. But the demonstrations had been held in full view of Western reporters and television cameras. Power had clearly moved to the streets.

After the protests in Berlin, we shifted our attention to Leipzig, where for three Mondays in a row people had been attending prayers in the St. Nicholas Church and then marching with candles through the streets. The marches were getting bigger by the week, and after what happened in Berlin, we expected tens of thousands to come out in Leipzig. Honecker expected them too, and unknown to us, he had had enough. His anniversary party had been ruined; demonstrators had raised riot in his capital, chanting the hated Soviet leader's name. It was time to get tough, to unleash the "Chinese solution." He ordered security forces to prepare to open fire. We later learned that machine guns were mounted on the main post office in anticipation of the march.

Visiting dignitaries observe the fortieth-anniversary festivities in East Berlin. Front row from left: Poland's Jaruselski, Romania's Ceausescu, Gorbachev of the Soviet Union, and Honecker of East Germany.

I watched the demonstration in Leipzig that Monday evening completely unaware of the danger. About 70,000 people, many with candles, marched peacefully around the Dittrichring, a broad street that went around the city center, chanting *Wir sind das Volk*—"We are the people." Security forces made no effort to stop them. Tens of thousands more marched in Dresden, Potsdam, and Magdeburg, all peacefully.

Later, after the wall came down, we learned about Honecker's orders, and we heard various versions of why they were not carried out. Egon Krenz, a member of the Politburo (the senior members of the Communist Party who ran East Germany), was in charge of security. He told reporters that he was the one who had countermanded Honecker. "I was in Leipzig. I helped there to see to it that these things were solved politically," he said. But Krenz said this when he was urgently trying to improve his image in order to stay in power. Another version of the story is that the initiative to avoid bloodshed came from Kurt Masur, the celebrated orchestra conductor who was then director of the Leipzig Gewandhaus Orchestra, and who had held an emergency meeting with Leipzig authorities. Yet another possibility is that the Soviet military commander intervened. Perhaps the current Russian president, Vladimir Putin, who was a KGB officer in East Germany at the time, will reveal the truth someday.

Teenagers burn the East German constitution during a protest in Leipzig in 1989.

However it happened, it was the turning point in Germany's peaceful revolution. The failure of the Communist Party to crush the protests meant the effective end of its authority. Without fear and force, the party had no way of controlling the people. On October 18, Honecker was fired and Krenz was named the new party chief. He lasted barely six weeks in the job. A few years later, Honecker, Krenz, and several other East German leaders were charged with the deaths of people who were shot trying to cross the wall. Honecker was released for reasons of health and moved to Chile, where he died in May 1994 of liver cancer. Krenz spent three years in prison and now lives in quiet retirement in Germany.

With the machinery of repression neutralized, the streets grew rapidly in power. A week later, 100,000 marched through Leipzig; a week after that, the number was 320,000. People in every city and town now began to hold mass meetings at which speakers denounced the ruling Communists. On November 4, half a million people marched through the streets of East Berlin in what Christa Wolf, a popular writer, now referred to as a "revolution from below." Nobody was afraid anymore. We wandered around interviewing people, and they spoke freely and happily. In fact, the four-hour rally was actually broadcast live on East German radio and television. Most of the placards, and most of the speakers, now demanded free speech, free elections, an end to the "leading role" of the Communist Party, and—a demand that got the loudest cheers—a settling of accounts with the despised security police.

One of the speakers was the writer Stefan Heym. "Dear friends and fellow citizens," he said, "this is as if a window has been thrown open after all the years of stagnation in spiritual, economic, and political life, after the years of stupefaction, the thrashing-out of phrases and bureaucratic arbitrariness, of official blindness, and deafness. What a transformation!"

In the surest sign that life had changed, there was also good humor aplenty. One of the last speakers on that day was a popular actress, Steffie Spira, who before leaving the podium raised a roar of laughter by saying, "I want the government to do what I am about to do. Step down."

After that, events moved quickly. The headlines in *The New York Times* track the accelerating story: "East Germans Declare Amnesty for Those Who Fled." "Another Big Rally in East Germany." "East Germans' New Leader Vows Far-Reaching Reform and Urges an End to Flight." "500,000 in East Germany Rally for Change." November 7: "A Draft Law Grants East Germans the Right to Travel or Emigrate." November 8: "East Germany's Cabinet Resigns, Bowing to Protest and Mass Flight."

And then, November 9.

A father and daughter (left) wear headbands bearing the slogan "No violence" at a protest in East Berlin.

SIX

The Berlin Wall Comes Tumbling Down

When I woke up in my West Berlin hotel that morning, I knew it would be a big day, but there was no way I could have guessed how big. East German officials had called a press conference, and we had heard that they were planning to announce changes in the despised Travel Law, which prevented East Germans from traveling to the West. The press conference was in East Berlin. That meant I had to cross the Berlin Wall.

Unlike the East Germans, I could cross the border anytime with my American passport. But it was not easy. There were only two crossing points for foreigners, one for crossing by train and one for cars. I always drove because I needed a car in East Berlin, and that meant passing through Checkpoint Charlie. The name Charlie came from the military alphabet—Checkpoints Alpha and Bravo were at either end of the highway from West Germany to West Berlin, and Checkpoint Charlie crossed from West Berlin into East Berlin on what had been one of the main streets of the old capital, Friedrichstrasse (Friedrich Street).

In the days before the wall fell, I made the crossing often—sometimes several times a day. Often there was a long line of cars waiting to get into the large roofed area, where East German guards carefully checked my passport and waited until I exchanged twenty-five West German marks (about fourteen dollars at the time) for twenty-five East German marks, which were worth a lot less and could be used only in East Germany. The exchange was a way for East Germany to get valuable Western currency— "real money"—that the government could use to buy things in the West.

The guards looked under the car with mirrors. Later, on the way out, they would even stick a long rod into the gas tank to make sure I wasn't smuggling someone out. It took at least half an hour to get through, more if there was a long line of cars.

I never got over the feelings of tension and irritation that came with entering a police state. There were no mobile phones then, so once I was through the checkpoint it was very difficult to make a telephone call back to the West. On the Eastern side, an American correspondent was regarded with suspicion, and I always assumed that I was being followed.

I drove through the checkpoint into the grayness of East Berlin, met Viktor, who served as my translator, and headed for the press conference.

There, Günter Schabowski, a member of the Politburo, announced that the government was introducing new regulations that would make it far easier and far quicker for East Germans to get permission to visit the West. But the way Schabowski phrased it left many questions unanswered.

"Personal travel abroad can be applied for without any extra requirements," he said. "The relevant passport and registration departments are instructed to promptly grant exit visas for permanent departure…" What did this mean? That anyone could get a permit anytime? Starting when? It would take some time to get the details straight, and I wanted to get back through Checkpoint Charlie before the other reporters, so I decided to go back to West Berlin as soon as the press conference was over. I figured the details would be on the radio later, and I wanted to get a head start on the story.

After I left—at 6:57 p.m., to be exact—Schabowski was besieged by reporters. Tom Brokaw, the NBC anchorman, asked Schabowski in English if he meant to say that the Berlin Wall was open. Schabowski did not speak English too well and probably did not fully understand the question. Whatever he thought it meant, he answered "Yes."

Günter Schabowski of the East German Politburo started a rush to the Berlin Wall with his announcement on November 9, 1989, that travel restrictions would be lifted.

Border guards hold back a crowd of excited spectators at the opening of the Berlin Wall.

That was it. Within minutes, West German television and radio were reporting that travel to the West was possible immediately. All West German stations deliberately beamed their broadcasts across the wall, and most East Berliners routinely tuned in to news from West Berlin. So the news swept through East and West Berlin, and beyond, like a grass fire. In Bonn, the news interrupted a debate in parliament and all the legislators rushed to television sets. Berliners on both sides dropped whatever they were doing to listen, and many spontaneously headed for the wall.

In East Berlin, an American diplomat was on his way home at ten p.m. He was amazed to find scores of little East German Trabant cars parked every which way near one of the wall crossings set up for Germans, as if the drivers had jumped out in a great rush. On the other side, Western television cameras had already gathered and had their lights trained at the crossing. The crowds rapidly grew to dangerous size. But the East German border troops had no orders, except the old ones, which were to shoot anyone trying to cross without authorization. Victor rushed to the Bornholmer Strasse crossing as soon as he heard the news on the radio and waited with the growing crowd as the border guards just stood around with their automatic rifles, unsure of what to do. People were squeezed right up against the barriers, and the push was getting worse by the minute.

The officer in charge realized that if this continued the people would either break through or be crushed. Finally, at 11:14 p.m., he gave what turned out to be a historic order: Throw open the gates! With the pent-up pressure of decades of division propelling them, thousands burst through the opening and into the arms of waiting West Germans. People wept, hugged, popped bottles of champagne. Victor was among the first ones through. A West German embraced him and tried to give him some champagne. But Victor pleaded with the man to take him to my hotel. He had never been to West Berlin and he had no idea where it was. Within minutes, he was pounding on my door.

On the first day after the wall opened, 800,000 East Germans came across. The party went on for days as millions of Berliners passed back and forth. Under West German law, every East German arriving in the West was entitled to a one-time gift of "welcome money"—*Begrüssungsgeld*—of one hundred marks, about fifty-four dollars at the time. Long lines formed at banks for what East Berliners believed was a princely sum, until they discovered what prices were like in the West. At the checkpoints, where border guards used to prod gas tanks and probe under seats for would-be escapees, the police now mingled happily with people going back and forth unhindered. "We were as surprised as everyone else," said one smiling guard. Amazingly, East Germans did not try to stay in the West. Almost all of them headed home after a day of shopping and partying, now certain that the wall would never be closed again.

Soon East Germans started coming across in their primitive Trabant and Wartburg cars. For the West Germans, whose cars were the best in the world, these small, stinky, and noisy cars were a joke, and they took to giving the Trabants, which are made of plastic and pressed wood, a few friendly slaps on the roof—"Trabi-thumping," we called it. West Germans also began crossing eastward, wandering through historic districts of East Berlin and discovering a Germany that had changed far less than the West, at least physically, since World War II.

The day after the wall opened, a young German participates in the latest craze, chipping a piece from the Berlin Wall to keep as a souvenir.

(Near right) A teenager shows her East German passport as she passes through the wall to visit West Berlin for the first time.

(Far right) Smiling East and West German border guards mingle with the crowds.

(Bottom) West Germans welcome travelers from the East by "thumping" the hood of their car.

People began to chip away at the hated wall. It became a national obsession: Break down the wall! Stores soon ran out of chisels and hammers. From my hotel I could hear the banging all night. One night, I went out myself and chipped away until I smashed my thumb. (Chunks of the wall are on sale to this day at souvenir shops in Berlin.)

The wave of freedom continued to move through Eastern Europe after that, sweeping over Bulgaria, Czechoslovakia, and finally Romania. I hopped around Eastern Europe all that year, witnessing the power of people who wanted to be free. One memory sticks out in particular. In November 1989 I was on the vast Wenceslas Square in Prague, the capital of Czechoslovakia. A light, wet snow was falling, but a quarter of a million people packed every inch of the square, all merrily jangling their keys to "ring out" the old regime.

There were violent clashes, to be sure, but for the most part it was bloodless. The exception was in Romania, which became the last of the Eastern European states to overthrow its Communists and the only one to do it brutally. Nicolae Ceausescu, the Romanian Communist dictator, had established a massive personality cult—his portrait hung on every billboard, and he maintained a ruthless control of his people through the Securitate, the secret police. He was not about to exit peacefully.

The revolution reached Romania late in 1989—on December 16, to be exact, when a government move against a dissident priest in the western city of Timisoara grew into mass protests and riots. The security forces crumbled before the onslaught, and Ceausescu and his wife, Elena, tried to flee. But they were captured and, on Christmas Day, 1989, shot by a ragtag bunch of soldiers.

96

98

Seven

How Many Germanys?

Citizens of Sibiu, Romania, light candles to honor the memory of people killed when security forces fired on antigovernment demonstrators in nearby Timisoara on December 17, 1989.

1989 was drawing to an end. It had been an extraordinarily exciting year. But I spent its last days in the sad task of traveling to Timisoara to evacuate a colleague from *The New York Times*, John Tagliabue, who had been shot and seriously wounded there. Again a wet, heavy snow was falling as I drove through the terrified, battered streets of the provincial city. There were bullet holes in many walls, and many candles were being lit for the dead and wounded at the Romanian Orthodox Cathedral. Across Eastern Europe, the people had won, but they had also suffered casualties.

The question now was "What next?"

At the end of World War II, the Allies had a plan. But in Eastern Europe, everything was happening so quickly, and so unexpectedly, that nobody had time to plan ahead. Country after country was throwing out Communist governments, but the cold war structures were still in place. The Warsaw Pact still existed, and the Soviet Union was still a mighty superpower. Hundreds of thousands of Soviet troops were stationed in East Germany, hundreds of thousands of American troops in West Germany.

Yet now that the wall was down, the same thought was on every German's mind, and it was best expressed by the tabloid *Bild* in a huge headline: "This Is the First Step to Unity!"

But what did *unity* mean? Some people thought the two Germanys should remain separate countries, loosely united in a confederation. Others argued that they should fully merge. Still others, mindful of World War II, worried that a reunited Germany could become dangerous again.

There were many reasons to resist a rush to reunification. The French, the British, the Russians, and many officials in the U.S. administration were reluctant to upset the East-West balance, which had brought four decades of peace to Europe. Officially, Western leaders were happy to see Communist governments overthrown. But the West had grown quite rich and happy during the cold war. The Americans and the Soviets had learned to manage their conflict, so the threat of a nuclear war was minimal. And with Gorbachev in power, they could expect relations to become even better. Reuniting Germany would upset the process.

Many East German intellectuals also opposed reunification. They believed that their country could build a form of democratic socialism that would retain social equality and avoid the worst aspects of Western capitalism. In his brief time in office, Egon Krenz had declared that the Communist Party would work toward "a revolution on German soil" that would bring "a socialism that is economically effective, politically democratic, morally clean, and will turn to the people in everything."

100

In West Germany, reunification had always been an official goal. In fact, the West German government never recognized the East German state and always officially held that Germany would become one again. But it was always a distant dream, something that would happen gradually and naturally. After the wall came down, many West Germans still believed that there was a long way to go before reunification.

Willy Brandt, a former West German chancellor who had been the mayor of West Berlin when the wall went up in 1961, told a rally in West Berlin shortly after the wall came down: "The moving together of the German states is taking shape in reality in a different way than many of us expected. No one should act as if he knows in which concrete form the people in these two states will find a new relationship. But that they will find a relationship, that they will come together in freedom, that is the important point."

The leader of the West German government at the time was Chancellor Helmut Kohl, a large, provincial politician from the conservative Christian Democratic Party. His popularity among West Germans was never very high, but he was a master politician. He understood that if he was seen to be rushing toward unification, West Germany's neighbors could become alarmed. So when he first appeared in Berlin after the wall came down, he proclaimed, "Long live a free German fatherland! Long live a united Europe!"

Kohl had always believed that Germany would become one again only in a united Europe. If all the European states came together in a union, they would create a guarantee against the sort of wars that had ravaged the continent earlier in the century. And once there was no longer a threat of war, he believed, the Germans would be allowed to reunite their nation.

But Kohl also saw this as a long process. He developed a ten-point plan that envisioned a partnership between East and West Germany, leading eventually to a federation within a united Europe.

But it was the people in the streets who were setting the timetable, not the leaders. It was they who had forced the Communist regimes out across Eastern Europe. And the Germans who had fled by the thousands to the West, who had marched by the hundreds of thousands in Leipzig, Dresden, and East Berlin, who had rushed weeping and laughing through the breach in the Berlin Wall on November 9—they were still on the march. Except now the same marchers who had chanted *"Wir sind das Volk"*—"We are the people"—were chanting *"Wir sind ein Volk"*—"We are one people."

The East German Communist leadership was in full retreat. It tried to negotiate with opposition leaders, it abandoned its claim to a "leading role" in society, but still the pressures grew. The official Communist Party

Both the United States and the Soviet Union had built a strong military presence in Germany.

(Near right) Soviet soldiers prepare to withdraw and return to Russia.

(Far right) American troops on maneuvers at the East/West German border in 1986.

(Bottom) Helmut Kohl (right) and Hans Modrow (left) are mobbed by reporters at their Inter-German Summit on December 10, 1989.

A flag-waving crowd in Dresden greets Helmut Kohl on his visit to East Germany on December 19, 1989.

newspaper, *Neues Deutschland*, which had, until then, loyally printed only what the leaders wanted it to, suddenly published an investigative series of reports about the lavish lifestyles and high corruption of party leaders. Some top leaders were said to have huge Swiss bank accounts: one had a sumptuous estate on the Baltic coast; another was making a fortune on illegal arms deals. The entire Politburo was forced to resign. Then the secret police was disbanded. The party was finished.

On December 18, 1989, Chancellor Kohl made his first trip to East Germany, traveling to Dresden to talk over some details of relations between the two states with Prime Minister Hans Modrow, who was the leader of East Germany now that the Communist Party had lost power, and to present his ten-point plan. It proved to be a decisive moment for Kohl, and for the Germans. The chancellor, who never got much public support in West Germany, was greeted at the memorial ruins of the Frauen Church by more than 10,000 people chanting "Helmut! Helmut!" He got the loudest cheers when he declared, "My goal, when the historic moment makes it possible, is the unity of our nation. I know we can reach this goal." At the end, Kohl wished the East Germans a happy Christmas, and then, his voice breaking, he concluded, "God bless our German fatherland."

On New Year's Eve, 1989, celebrating Germans sing together at the Brandenburg Gate.

It was on that day in Dresden, Kohl told me later, that he realized he could not delay the reunification of his country. From this point on, his goal would be to unify Germany as quickly as possible.

And so 1989 came to an end. Back from Romania, I took my family to Berlin to greet the New Year. The party was spectacular. "I partook of history," wrote my young son in an awed report for his class after a night of fireworks, champagne, and chipping for pieces of the wall.

Watching the crowds mingling easily at the Brandenburg Gate, it was hard to believe that this was the same place to which we had rushed less than three months earlier to watch the first East Germans pouring through. The wall, the guard towers, the barbed wire, were gone. So was the fear. It was obvious that reunification would not wait.

EIGHT
Reunited!

Several weeks after the Berlin Wall was breached, I came upon a sad and strange story. For years, rabbits had made a home in the no man's land where the wall divided into parallel lines of concrete barriers. The rabbits weren't heavy enough to set off land mines, and the patrol dogs were always on leashes, so the rabbits grew up with no natural enemies. On the contrary, the people who climbed onto platforms built for visitors on the Western side of the wall threw lettuce and other food to the rabbits. They lived in a rabbit's paradise— well fed, totally secure, and with plenty of room to hop around.

When holes opened up in the wall, the rabbits hopped out. Out in the real world, many got run over by cars or eaten by dogs. Many others probably perished simply from not knowing how to find food on their own. To me, the plight of the rabbits was the plight of many East Germans. They had been raised in a system that planned their lives from cradle to grave and kept them walled up. They had little preparation for the rough, competitive world of capitalism, and few defenses against the allure of glittering Western consumer goods. Their factories were no match for modern West German industries, and their East German marks weren't worth a lot. Most of them spent their fifty-five dollars' worth of West German "welcome money" almost immediately.

Many years later, when West Germany was suffering from the enormous cost of reunification, many Germans wondered whether it had been the right thing to do, or whether it could have been done differently. But at the time, the hard fact was that West Germany had no choice but to absorb East Germany, and to absorb it quickly. With no wall in the way, the East Germans once again began migrating west at an alarming rate—60,000 a month. The East German economy was failing, its currency had to be replaced, and its 17 million citizens had to be rapidly incorporated into the West German economy. Other Eastern European countries could plod along on their old industries, but East Germany simply could not continue as a poor and bedraggled cousin alongside a rich West Germany. It was a helpless and threatened rabbit, and it had to be rescued.

106

I visited Magdeburg, a grimy industrial city in East Germany, in late January 1990. Factories were already laying off workers, something unthinkable in the old state of workers and peasants. Pensioners and unskilled laborers were worried about their benefits. There were still weekly demonstrations, but the signs were no longer "Unity" or "Communists Out," but "Protect Our Social Benefits" and "No Unemployment." Basically, everybody was waiting for the West Germans to take over. In fact, some West Germans were already there, but they were mostly hunting for bargains and opportunities to make quick money. I collared one sleek West German who drove up in a Jaguar. "I probably shouldn't talk to you," he said with a wink, "but I'm here to set up a casino and some video-game parlors."

Once again the popular revolution was taking its own course, independent of what politicians preferred. Everybody in East Germany now recognized that union with West Germany was inevitable, near, and necessary. And the longer it was delayed, the uglier it could become.

Chancellor Helmut Kohl understood this, and he moved quickly. Early that year, he persuaded the East Germans to move national elections to an earlier date and threw his considerable weight behind pro-unification groups. Kohl campaigned in East Germany as if he were on his home turf. "We are one Germany. We are one people," he proclaimed at every stop, basking in the roar of "Helmut! Helmut!" He succeeded, and the only free elections the East Germans ever held produced a government pledged to dissolve the state. Talks began immediately on economic and currency union, the first step toward unification. "Every day we waste not having reunification just makes matters worse," said Susanna Frank, a twenty-five-year-old East Berliner, echoing a common sentiment among voters.

The first real change for the East Germans came on July 1, when at the stroke of midnight East Germany turned its economy and currency over to West Germany. It was an amazing feat, done with German efficiency: 15,000 special distribution centers across East Germany opened promptly at eight a.m. to allow East Germans to swap their nearly worthless currency for the strong West German mark at the rate of one to one. Children could change up to 2,000 East German marks, adults up to 4,000, senior citizens up to 6,000. All salaries and benefits were switched to West German marks.

108

Helmut Kohl smiles for the camera on a campaign tour in 1990.

Because the East German mark was worth a lot less than the West German mark in the world market, the exchange amounted to a massive financial gift to the East Germans. While they were working for East German money, the East German laborers had been, in effect, working for a lot less pay than comparable West German workers. Now, West Germany was paying them far higher wages to do the same work. The problem was that this made their products far more expensive, and many of their factories could no longer compete in the global market. Many of them closed down, putting people out of work. To this day, eastern Germany has a far higher unemployment rate than western Germany, and subsidies for eastern Germany drain huge resources from the German economy.

East Berlin teens drape themselves in East German flags as a statement against reunification during the March 1990 elections.

Some economists argue today that the currency exchange was a huge mistake. Others say it was the most practical way to quickly unite the East and West German economies. Personally, I cannot see that there was much choice at the time. Why would East Germans have stayed home if that meant working for far lower wages than they could get in the West?

The diplomatic obstacles to reunification were even greater. Mikhail Gorbachev had not interfered when the wall came down. But he had

A woman casts her ballot in the East German elections of March 1990. Voters elected a government that pledged to dissolve itself and reunify with West Germany.

Helmut Kohl (left) visits with the first President Bush (right) at the White House in 1990.

assumed that East Germany would remain a separate state allied to Moscow, and he certainly did not want East Germany to become part of NATO, which it would if it was absorbed into West Germany. Gorbachev had been furious when Kohl announced his ten-point unity plan in December. "Perhaps he thinks that his melody, the melody of his march, is already playing, and he is already marching to it," Gorbachev grumbled. Britain's prime minister, Margaret Thatcher, was equally opposed to reunification, as was President François Mitterrand of France. Neither of them wanted to upset the existing East-West balance, and both were wary of allowing Germany to become large and strong again.

The only international support for reunification—and it was key—came from the American president, George H. W. Bush. Even before the wall came down, President Bush had surprised allies when he said, "I don't share the concern that some European countries have about a reunified Germany." President Bush felt that reunification was unavoidable and that it was best to do it quickly—and with American support. The United States, the president wrote to Chancellor Kohl, would not allow the Soviet Union "to force [them] to create the kind of Germany Moscow might want, at the pace Moscow might prefer."

In the end, Gorbachev relented. On July 16, Kohl flew to the

Caucasus resort of Zheleznovodsk, near Gorbachev's hometown of Stavropol, where Gorbachev agreed to let a united Germany join NATO, and to eventually pull Soviet troops out of Germany. Part of the agreement required Germany to give considerable financial aid to the Soviet Union. I remember watching Kohl during the press conference— he could not stop smiling. The way was clear.

October 3 was set as the date for unification. Nobody thought any longer of partnerships or federations; the plan was simply for East Germany and its 16 million citizens to be absorbed into West Germany, retaining the constitution, the laws, the government, the anthem, and the name of the Federal Republic of Germany. Nothing would be left of the German Democratic Republic.

Not all East Germans were happy at this prospect. At the Kartoon, a cabaret in East Berlin, one skit had a West German chicken proposing a joint venture to an East German pig.

"Let's make ham and egg sandwiches," proposed the Western chicken.

"Wait a minute—that means I have to die," protested the Eastern pig.

"Hey, it's not my fault you can't make eggs," said the chicken.

In September, the Soviet Union, the Western Allies, and the two Germanys cleared the last formal obstacle to unification, signing a treaty that ended the forty-five years of occupation that had followed World War II and left the two Germanys as sovereign nations. By now this was a simple formality, and the signing ceremony went almost unnoticed.

And so, at the stroke of midnight on Tuesday, October 2, 1990, less than a year after the wall fell open, the two Germanys became one again and Berlin became once again the political and spiritual capital of Germany. A replica of the American Liberty Bell, a gift from the United States at the height of the cold war, tolled from the town hall, and the black, red, and gold banner of what had been West Germany rose slowly before the Reichstag, the scarred seat of past German parliaments, now the flag of all Germany.

Drawing on the words of the West German constitution, the German president Richard von Weizsäcker proclaimed from the steps of the Reichstag: "In free self-determination, we want to achieve the unity in freedom of Germany. We are aware of our responsibility for these tasks before God and the people. We want to serve peace in the world in a united Europe." At the same time, the first and last democratically elected leader of East Germany, Prime Minister Lothar de Maizière, committed his country to history with the words "It is the end of many illusions. It is a farewell without tears."

The Berlin Wall was down for good, the partying was done, and I wish I could write that the Germans lived happily ever after. But reunification was only the beginning of a new and difficult period. Already, by the time the formal reunification took place, West Germans were grumbling at the huge cost of absorbing the "Ossies," and the East Germans were angry at being treated as second-class citizens by the "Wessies." For some people, reunification turned out to be a disaster. In at least one case, a West German businessman who had had dealings on both sides of the wall had established separate families in each Germany, who suddenly discovered each other.

Neo-Nazis take part in an antigovernment protest in Berlin on November 25, 2000.

In 1992, the Stasi's secret files were opened for inspection. Many people were revealed to have been secret agents or spies—including a West Berliner I had often used as a guide and a source. He had always been useful and well informed, and it turned out that he had been a Soviet spy. He was sentenced to three years in prison for that.

In general, reunification proved to be enormously costly and difficult. In the forty years that they were divided, the two Germanys had become very different, and the Communist-trained East German officials, ranging from judges and administrators to teachers, had to be retrained or replaced. The entire East German infrastructure—telephones, highways—had to be modernized. Many East German enterprises proved to be too obsolete, or too expensive, to run and were simply shut down. The persisting unemployment in the east has fed widespread resentment against western Germans and against immigrants, and has led to an upsurge of neo-Nazi violence.

Many western Germans (we don't say West Germans or East Germans anymore) blame the tens of billions of dollars spent on propping up eastern Germany for the worst economic slump in Germany since the end of World War II. Many eastern Germans, for their part, have developed a sense of nostalgia for the cradle-to-grave security of their former state. They call it *ostalgia*, "eastalgia."

Still, the fall of the Berlin Wall remains one of the greatest outbursts of joy in history, and the reunification of Germany a remarkable feat. However great the troubles, for many Germans it has been the realization of their most cherished wish, which was best expressed by Helmut Kohl when he said that his greatest hope for his people now was simply that Germany would become accepted as normal.

And for some East Germans, the story *has* ended happily. Today, my old assistant, Victor, is the manager of the *New York Times* bureau in reunified Berlin.

Victor Homola, of the *New York Times* Berlin bureau, watches his daughter as she climbs a niche made in the Berlin Wall by souvenir collectors in 1989.

Postscript

(Far left)
Demonstrators
toppled a statue
in front of KGB
headquarters
in Moscow on
August 23, 1991.

(Near left)
Soviet leader
Mikhail Gorbachev,
with the Kremlin
in the background.

(Bottom)
Fireworks over
Red Square mark
the end of the
Soviet Union on
December 31, 1991.

After all the Eastern European dominoes fell, there was still one standing—the first one, the Soviet Union.

Mikhail Gorbachev had started the dominoes tumbling. But his purpose in launching glasnost and perestroika had been to prop up his own piece; to modernize and revive the Communist system, not to kill it. He really believed that the system could be made free and efficient, even though every country that had adopted it, from Cuba through China, had ended up with a totalitarian government. Gorbachev understood that if the system was not changed, it would die, but he failed to understand that once the props of terror and force were pulled out, it would collapse. Erich Honecker understood that, and so did the old Chinese leaders, and so did hard-line Soviet leaders who tried first to block Gorbachev and then to overthrow him.

Many of us who closely followed events in the Soviet Union— journalists, diplomats, intelligence agencies—were caught off-guard by how quickly the system crumbled. We knew that the Soviet economy was creaky, and that the Eastern Europeans were unhappy. But we were convinced that these highly militarized police states would do whatever they had to do to maintain control, the way the Chinese did at Tiananmen Square, or the way Kim Jong-il does to this day in North Korea, or Fidel Castro in Cuba.

Once Gorbachev opened the door to the yearnings of the people, however, they could not be stopped. Before long, the revolution that had swept through Eastern Europe was at his doorstep. First the Baltic States rebelled, then other republics and regions of the Soviet Union began to demand more freedom. In the uncertainty and chaos, the economy rapidly deteriorated, and people began lining up for basic food and supplies. Hailed as a savior when he came to power, Gorbachev steadily lost his popularity and support. In August 1991, hard-line Communists staged a coup in Moscow, but the rebellion collapsed. Now there was nothing to prevent the final dissolution of the old Soviet empire. In December 1991, Russia, Ukraine, and Belarus proclaimed an end to the Soviet state, and on December 25, 1991, Gorbachev resigned. The Soviet state ceased to exist.

By then, I had finished my assignment in Germany and was living in Moscow again. My children were visiting for Christmas, and they were walking around Red Square with my wife under a light snow. The great square is the heart of Russia. The ramparts of the Kremlin, the seat of Russian government, form one side and the whimsical St. Basil's Cathedral, with its colorful onion domes, forms another. Major military parades are held there, and the mummified body of Lenin, the founder of the Soviet Union, still lies on public display in a temple-like mausoleum.

I was in the office when my wife called. The old Soviet flag was coming down over the Kremlin, and the white, blue, and red flag of pre-revolutionary Russia was going up. I glanced at my watch: 7:32 p.m. That evening, I wrote an obituary for the Soviet Union:

MOSCOW - The Soviet state, marked throughout its brief but tumultuous history by great achievement and terrible suffering, died today after a long and painful decline. It was seventy-four years old.

Conceived in utopian promise and born in the violent upheavals

(Center) A field of crosses memorializing those killed at the Berlin Wall was dismantled in 2005.

(Left) Sections of the dismantled Berlin Wall a year after it fell.

of the "Great October Revolution of 1917," the union heaved its last
in the dreary darkness of late December 1991, stripped of ideology,
dismembered, bankrupt, and hungry—but awe-inspiring even in its fall.

The end of the Soviet Union came with the resignation of Mikhail
Gorbachev to make way for a new "Commonwealth of Independent States."
At 7:32 p.m., shortly after the conclusion of his televised address, the red flag
with hammer and sickle was lowered over the Kremlin and the white, blue,
and red Russian flag rose in its stead.

There was no ceremony, only the tolling of chimes from the Spassky
Gate, cheers from a handful of surprised foreigners, and an angry tirade
from a lone war veteran.

Many years have passed now, and the separate parts of the old Soviet
empire have had differing fates. All of the former Eastern European
countries are now members of NATO, and most of them have joined or are
in line to join the European Union. Russia itself has had considerable ups
and downs. A chaotic privatization program left many national resources in
the hands of a group of fabulously rich tycoons, and for years the country
has been mired in a war with the breakaway province of Chechnya.
President Vladimir Putin, elected with a huge vote, has made many Western
governments nervous with his drive to centralize power and control in the
Kremlin again.

(Right) Traffic flows freely through the Brandenburg Gate in reunified Berlin.

I went back to visit Berlin in November 2004, fifteen years after
the wall came down. The only hint left of the wall was a line of
paving stones that traced its path through the heart of the bustling
city. The line crossed sidewalks and streets, and sometimes
disappeared into glittering new office blocks. On Friedrichstrasse,
at the site of the old Checkpoint Charlie, there was a museum
about the Berlin Wall and a bunch of souvenir shops. Between
the Brandenburg Gate and the Reichstag, which again housed the
German parliament, stood crosses commemorating the people
who died trying to cross the wall. Now it was hard to find where
the wall had stood.

ARTICLES

East German teenagers played a large part in the demonstrations that eventually led to the opening of the Berlin Wall. A protest that broke out in 1987 after East German police attempted to break up a large crowd underscored the frustrations that teens felt in East Berlin.

RALLYING CRY OF EAST BERLINERS

By Serge Schmemann
West Berlin, June 9, 1987

Thousands of East German youths who skirmished with the police for the last three nights when barred from eavesdropping on rock concerts on the other side of the Berlin Wall chanted "The wall must go!" and a surprising new cry, "Gorbachev! Gorbachev!"

The latter chant, in front of the Soviet embassy, reflected the popular following that Mikhail S. Gorbachev and his calls for a new openness have attracted among East German youths and intellectuals.

Today, with no further rock concerts scheduled by the wall, the boulevard in front of the Brandenburg Gate was quiet, with only the usual clusters of tourists along the staunch barriers that delineate the no man's land between East and West Berlin in which the gate stands.

But witnesses to the demonstrations and confrontations that had racked the broad Unter den Linden boulevard leading up to the gate said East Berlin had seen nothing like it since a rock concert ten years earlier—that one inside East Berlin—touched off rioting by the fired-up audience.

The official East German press agency today denied the confrontations, saying: "There can be no talk at all of clashes between youths and police. These exist only in the fantasy of foreign correspondents who drive over the border with the aim of creating sensations."

Fifty Reported Arrested

At one point, some youths in the crowd sang the *Internationale*, the international Communist anthem, but the intent was apparently sarcastic.

Witnesses said the fiercest clashes took place after eleven p.m., when uniformed and plainclothes police waded into one group of demonstrators with truncheons, hauling many off to paddy wagons. Witnesses said at least fifty youths were arrested, many raising their fingers in the V sign as they were driven off.

West German television said one of its crews was assailed by the police, who drove the cameraman into a nearby courtyard and beat him badly. A West German radio reporter's equipment was smashed.

Throughout the furor, the rock concert by the British group Genesis, which was taking place on the field in front of the old Reichstag building on the west side of the wall, was barely audible, but many of the East German youths carried portable radios on which the concert could be heard.

East German teenagers on their way to a rock concert in 1987.

On December 10, 1989, The New York Times *ran several articles that captured the excitement of Berliners when the wall came down. This one described the jubilant crowds that had poured through the wall the day before.*

EAST GERMANY OPENS FRONTIER TO THE WEST

By Serge Schmemann
East Berlin, November 10, 1989

East Germany on Thursday lifted restrictions on emigration or travel to the West, and within hours tens of thousands of East and West Berliners swarmed across the infamous Berlin Wall for a boisterous celebration.

Border guards at the Bornholmer Strasse crossing, Checkpoint Charlie, and several other crossings abandoned all efforts to check credentials, even though the new regulations said East Germans would still need passports and permission to get across. Some guards smiled and took snapshots, assuring passersby that they were just recording a historic event.

Politburo Announcement

The mass crossing began about two hours after Günter Schabowski, a member of the Politburo, had announced at a press conference that permission to travel or emigrate would be granted quickly and without preconditions, and that East Germans would be allowed to cross at any crossing into West Germany or West Berlin.

Flag Waving in the West

Once Schabowski's announcement was read on radio and television, a tentative trickle of East Germans testing the new regulations quickly turned into a jubilant horde, which joined at the border crossings with crowds of flag-waving, cheering West Germans. Thousands of Berliners clambered across the wall at the Brandenburg Gate, passing through the historic arch that for so long had been inaccessible to Berliners of either side.

Similar scenes were reported in Lubeck, the only other East German city touching the border, and at other border crossings along the inter-German frontier.

All through the night and into the early morning, celebrating East Berliners filled the Kürfurstendamm, West Berlin's

Berliners celebrate on the wall in November 1989, a few days after it opened.

"great white way," blowing trumpets, dancing, laughing, and absorbing a glittering scene that until now they could glimpse only on television.

Many East Germans said they planned to return home the same night. The mayor of West Berlin, Walter Momper, toured border crossings in a police radio truck and urged East Berliners to return.

East German radio announced that the uncontrolled crossings would be ended at eight a.m. today, after which East Germans would be required to obtain a visa.

With help from those on top, East Berliners climb the wall near the Brandenburg Gate.

The extraordinary breach of what had been the most infamous stretch of the iron curtain marked the culmination of an extraordinary month that has seen the virtual transformation of East Germany under the dual pressures of unceasing flight and continuing demonstrations. It also marked a breach of a wall that had become the premier symbol of Stalinist oppression and of the divisions of Europe and Germany into hostile camps after World War II.

1871

In 1871, Germany was first unified under Otto Van Bismarck. There have been several Germanys over the 135 years since the country first became a single national unit, governed from Berlin. They have in turn stretched over widely varying territories, incorporated different peoples, and erected different political systems.

The Germany forged in war and diplomacy by Bismarck stretched in the west from Alsace and Lorraine, seized in a war with France in 1870, to the territories of East Prussia, now parts of either Poland or Russia. Bismarck's Germany had some fundamental features that have endured throughout modern history. It had the largest population in Europe, outside Russia; it had the continent's most powerful economy; and it had the most advanced system of social welfare in Europe.

1919

The Germany that remained after World War I, the second of the modern Germanys, was vastly changed in its size and extent from Bismarck's era, though, internally, much remained unaltered. The last emperor, Wilhelm II, abdicated, and what became known as the Weimar Republic was formed two days before Germany surrendered. In the peace treaty imposed by the Allies, Germany gave back Alsace and Lorraine to the French. Poland was created from territory formerly held by Germany, Russia, and Austria-Hungary.

Poland got large portions of previously German territory, including a corridor to the sea and the mining territory of Upper Silesia.

Germany was reduced, but it was also left without a counterbalance in central Europe, because the old Austrian, Ottoman, and Russian Empires had been carved up.

1943

At the height of Hitler's conquests, Nazi Germany incorporated large areas of Eastern and central Europe into the Third Reich, including Austria and western Czechoslovakia, which were seized before war broke out, and large parts of western Poland, which was overrun in 1939. The Greater German Reich was the heart of a plan for dominating Europe that also included areas under occupation like France, satellites like Hungary, and Slavic regions in the east.

1945

After World War II, Germany's borders were dramatically redrawn. The border of Poland was moved about 100 miles to the west to compensate for Polish lands taken in the war by the Soviet Union. The former German territory of East Prussia was divided between Poland and the Soviet Union. The four occupation zones later became East and West Germany

1990

With reunification, East Germany (the German Democratic Republic) and West Germany (the Federal Republic of Berlin) were combined to form one nation under the laws and government of the Federal Republic of Germany, with Berlin as its capital.

Allied leaders meet at Yalta, February 1945.
From left: British prime minister Winston Churchill,
American president Franklin D. Roosevelt, and
Soviet premier Joseph Stalin.

THE BITTER LEGACY OF YALTA: FOUR DECADES OF WHAT-IFS

By Jason DeParle
November 26, 1989

For half a century, "Yalta" was one of the most charged words in the American political vocabulary—a potent symbol that critics used to conjure sins from gross naiveté to outright treason. Roosevelt himself died two months after the conference, but his admirers have never finished defending his reputation from the accusation that Yalta gave too much of Eastern Europe to Stalin.

The word "Yalta" was often a political shorthand for events that both preceded and followed the meetings in that Soviet city on the Black Sea in February 1945 among Roosevelt, Stalin, and Churchill. Perhaps unfairly, the word was used to signify the postwar division of Europe.

The agreements reached at Yalta were these: The Allies settled on a military strategy for concluding the war and restated plans to divide Germany into zones of occupation. They scheduled a conference to prepare the United Nations charter. In a secret agreement, they decided that the Soviet Union would enter the war against Japan in exchange for railway rights in Manchuria and territorial concessions. In addition, the Allies signed a Declaration on Liberated Europe endorsing "the right of all peoples to choose the form of government under which they live" through "democratic means" and "free elections."

Perhaps the most difficult problem tackled at Yalta, and the center of the outcry later, was the fate of postwar Poland. The occupying Red Army had installed a loyal provisional government; the issue was whether Churchill and Roosevelt could sway the Soviets to include non-Communist Polish leaders. Stalin agreed to hold "free and unfettered elections," but the Western leaders failed to find a way to guarantee enforcement. The agreement was initially hailed at home. A *New York Times* editorial said it offered "new life to the ideals of liberty and democracy." But it soon became clear that the Soviets, far from broadening the Polish government, were tightening their control. Thus emerged Poland: unfree and fettered.

Facts on the Ground

With the fact of Soviet domination came the accusation that Roosevelt had senselessly surrendered freedom—Poland's in particular and Eastern Europe's generally.

Defenders of the agreement point to the facts on the ground: the Red Army controlled Poland and was forty miles from Berlin, while the Allies in the West had yet to cross the Rhine. "Roosevelt didn't give Stalin Eastern Europe; Stalin had taken Eastern Europe," said James MacGregor Burns, a Roosevelt biographer. "They had the bodies on the soil." In the view of Roosevelt's admirers, his bargaining ability was limited not just by the position of the Red Army but also by his need to win Stalin's cooperation in realms beyond Eastern Europe. Roosevelt, who did not know whether the atomic bomb would work, felt he would need Soviet help against Japan as well as Germany.

Roosevelt was also determined to secure Stalin's participation in the United Nations. In

that context, Roosevelt's defenders say, securing Soviet endorsement of free Polish elections was the best he could do. But Roosevelt's critics say his priorities were mistaken, as in his stress on the United Nations, and that he was naive about Stalin, whose contempt for democracy had been well demonstrated. They also note that there was strong evidence that the Red Army was responsible for the murder of about 4,250 non-Communist Polish officers, the heart of any future resistance.

While Roosevelt may not have been able to change Stalin's military advantage in the East, the Yalta critics say, he could have condemned the Soviet leader's territorial designs—particularly in the weeks after Yalta, when they started to become clearer and Churchill urged him to confront Stalin directly. A more vigorous diplomacy might have heartened the democratic opposition and slowed Stalin, these critics say, and this would have left more of Europe free.

Protestors throw rocks at a Soviet tank during the East German uprising of 1953. Critics contend that the Yalta Agreement cleared the way for Soviet domination of Eastern Europe.

While every Warsaw Pact country was considered a "sovereign state"—one that determined its own policy —the Soviet government in Moscow controlled events in each of its satellite states through direct contact, military forces, and large contingents of secret agents. Written shortly after the pact was signed, this article outlined some of the ways by which the Soviet Union maintained control of East Germany.

THE "SOVEREIGNTY" OF EAST GERMANY

By Walter Sullivan
Berlin, December 10, 1955

On September 20, the Soviet Union transferred to East Germany control over all traffic between Berlin and West Germany except that of the United States, British, and French forces stationed in the city. The East German regime now is using this control as a lever to force the West to recognize it as a sovereign government.

Puppet State

West Germany is reluctant to do so on the ground that East Germany is a puppet state that cannot be said to represent the people of that region.

What is the nature of this state, which rules 17.5 million persons and demands acceptance as a sovereign government?

In structure the government appears to be completely independent. With the termination of the office of the Soviet High commissioner September 20, the last overt symbol of Soviet supervision vanished.

It is through the East German Communist party, known as the Socialist Unity Party, that Soviet political influence is exercised in East Germany. It is believed this is done only on the highest level. At the lower levels there is little contact between Soviet and East German officials.

East German policy is decided by the Politburo of the Socialist Unity Party. Politburo members hold key government posts and are thus responsible also for important day-to-day decisions. They are in constant contact with Soviet officials.

Despite this limited area of direct contact, East Germany is probably less independent than any country of the Soviet Bloc. There have been dissident elements within the Communist movement who wanted to devise a "German way" to socialism rather than slavishly imitate the Soviet Union, but there never has been any real threat of an open break with Moscow.

Such a split with the Soviet leadership is inconceivable in East Germany, whereas Moscow has regarded such action as a real danger in neighboring countries.

The East German Democratic Republic is in fact fundamentally different from other states in the Soviet Bloc.

Different Status

Its special status is acknowledged by the Communists, who do not class it as a "people's democracy," although that term is applied to other Eastern European countries. East Germany thus is viewed as being at an earlier stage of development toward socialism.

Its structure is similar to that of the "people's democracies," with a cabinet governing by decree. A People's Parliament gives token approval after decrees already have gone into effect but it has no real policymaking function. There are non-Communist parties but the Communists control and direct the entire political structure. Elections are consulted on a one-list system—only one candidate runs for each office, with no rivalry between candidates.

East Germany is almost certainly the weakest state of the Soviet Bloc and this tends to increase its dependence on Moscow.

In contrast to other Eastern European countries, where native Communists stepped into government roles, there were few Communists living in East Germany to form the nucleus of a new regime. Many had fled the country before World War II, when the Nazi party declared Communists to be enemies of the German people. Those who came back from exile in the Soviet Union or the West had lost contact with the people of their country.

The riots of June 17, 1953, demonstrated the unpopularity of the regime. Such an uprising is unlikely to recur so long as Soviet troops remain in the country. More than 300,000 are believed to be there now.

The East German ground forces number only about 95,000 men, with an added 15,000 in naval and air units. These armed forces are still technically classed as the people's police.

It is significant that they are under much closer Soviet surveillance than is the political structure. Soviet liaison officers are said to be stationed with each unit down to the company level.

Militia Formed

In an attempt to achieve greater stability, the East German regime began in 1953 to form militia units in all large factories and government offices. They are known as Kampfgruppen, or fighting groups, and are reminiscent of those in the Czechoslovak factories, which violently crushed a coup in 1948. The East German fighting groups are believed to number more than 100,000.

The groups are designed to prevent a repetition of the revolts of industrial workers throughout East Germany in 1953. The membership is drawn from the more loyal workers.

To some extent those fighting groups symbolize the instability of the East German government. Nevertheless, there has been a marked decline in internal resistance to the Communists. A large part of the opposition has fled to West Germany. The secret police force has rooted out and jailed many other opponents.

Few Key Men

Arrayed against the remaining dissidents are workers, youths, and the intelligentsia—the intellectual elite—who have been won over by the Communists. They probably constitute only a small proportion of the total but they generally are in key positions.

One of the subtlest elements weakening the East German government, and one that has its influence in Bonn as well, is the fact that it governs only part of a divided country. The question of how long this government will last is in the minds of East German officials, as well as of the populace.

The construction of the Berlin Wall sparked a diplomatic crisis between the free West and Communist East. But it was also a personal tragedy for thousands of Berlin residents, as they found themselves suddenly separated from family and friends by fences, barbed wire, and armed guards. The New York Times captured some of those people's stories in an article published in 1961, four days after the wall was first erected.

A father and mother hold up their children so grandparents across the Berlin Wall can see them.

BERLINERS GATHER AT BARRICADE

Berlin, August 23, 1961

There was a wedding in Berlin yesterday. The bride and bridegroom and some of their friends and the minister stood in West Berlin, just by the wall that the Communists have built to separate West Berlin from Communist East Berlin.

The mother of the bride stood on the other side of the wall, in East Berlin, crying. This and a hundred other tragedies, small when put up against the big issues involved, are what the splitting of the city means.

A Fatal Leap

The Communist police nailed wooden boards across the front door of Frau Ida Siekmann's house, one of the hundreds that stand on East Berlin territory with their front doors facing sidewalks that are in West Berlin. The police also boarded up windows on the first and second floors.

Frau Siekmann, fifty-nine years old, climbed to the third floor. She opened a window, threw some belongings and her papers on the West Berlin sidewalk, and jumped. She died in the ambulance on the way to the hospital.

Cemetery Blocked

An East Berlin woman died on Friday and her body was taken for burial the following Sunday to the East Berlin cemetery. But the entrance to the cemetery is in West Berlin.

Saturday night, the border was closed. The burial took place on schedule as the widower looked over the cemetery wall and the woman's West Berlin relatives tried to see through the gate.

"Tomorrow" Is Too Late

At the corner of Ocnkenstrasse and Harzerstrasse, two fifteen-year-old girls who had grown up together talked over what the West Berliners call the "Chinese wall" in the middle of the street.

"Tomorrow at the same time," one of the girls said. That night the height of the wall was raised to six feet.

"What Has Happened?"

Six East Berlin children are in West Berlin's West End Hospital. The doctors sent a message to the parents of one saying: "Operation successful but condition of your child still gives cause for worry."

The telegram was sent three times. The hospital received one telegram from the parents in East Berlin. It said: "What has happened? Answer immediately."

Ordeal of a Father

A couple of days before the border was closed, a family of eleven decided to try to escape on the elevated railway that used to carry thousands of Berliners back and forth daily across the two halves of the city.

The grandmother in the family took two boys, six and five years old. Eleven-year-old Petra went on a second train with her year-old brother in a baby carriage. Two boys, aged ten and nine, went on the same train as Petra, but in a different compartment. The parents and two other children took a third train.

All but Petra and the baby made it. The little girl and her brother were seized by the police before the train reached West Berlin.

"What should we do?" the father asked. "If we go back, we'll go to prison for fleeing. If we don't—" He went back the next day.

Tears in the West

A newsman came upon a young man near the border, staring intently into East Berlin with binoculars.

"See anyone you know?" the reporter asked jokingly.

"My fiancée," the man replied, turning away to hide his tears.

Roses in the East

On a street in East Berlin today, a French newspaperwoman was walking. An old man came up to her and thrust a bouquet of red roses into her hands. "Take these," he said, "and don't forget us. Don't forget us."

A woman stands on a stepladder and waves to East Berlin. In the early days of the wall this was a common way to keep in touch.

The death of Peter Fechter on August 17, 1962, sparked outrage in the West. Dozens of East Germans had already been killed trying to escape across the wall, but Peter Fechter's death struck a chord with West Berliners, who were unable to come to his aid when he called for help. Thousands of West Berlin residents turned out for a memorial service held in his honor. As a result of the shooting, an agreement was made to allow an ambulance to stand by on the Western side of the Friedrichstrasse crossing so that the West could aid any injured refugees fleeing from East Germany. This story from The New York Times *captures the indignation felt by Westerners.*

GERMAN REDS SHOOT FLEEING YOUTH

By Harry Gilroy

Berlin, August 17, 1962

East German border guards shot down a young man fleeing to West Berlin today and allowed him to lie dying for more than an hour at the foot of the Communists' wall dividing the city. A fellow refugee hurled himself over the barrier to safety. A crowd of West Berliners gathered at the wall shouting "Murderers!" at the East German guards. The guards then hurled tear-gas grenades at the crowd. The West Berlin police said

Peter Fechter lies dying on the Eastern side of the Berlin Wall after he was shot down while attempting to escape.

An hour and a half after Fechter was shot, East German policemen finally remove his body.

the two fleeing men, both eighteen years old, ran for the wall at 2:10 p.m., at a point where the Markgrafenstrasse runs into the barrier at the Zimmerstrasse.

This is two blocks east of the Friedrichstrasse crossing point where foreigners are checked in to and out of East Berlin.

The first the West Berlin police knew of the incident was when one of the young men was seen leaping over the wall while machine-gun fire broke out from two points.

The refugee who got across was cut by the barbed wire at the top of the six-foot barrier but was otherwise unhurt. His identity was not revealed.

From observation points the West Berlin police saw the second young man clinging to the wall. Then another shot struck him in the back and he fell.

He cried for help, but the West Berlin police could only throw bandages to him. Several times he cried out then lay still.

The rescue of the wounded man would have been possible only if the Communist guards had been fired on by the West Berlin police. But the police are under orders not to fire at the East German guards unless shots come into West Berlin, and that did not happen.

The East German guards watched from two concrete blockhouses with their guns directed toward the dying man.

It was 3:40 p.m. before a group of the guards hurried through the barbed wire and took the limp figure back into East Berlin. He was apparently dead. (The East German Interior Ministry said he had died in a hospital, United Press International reported.)

On April 15, 1989, protestors gathered in Tiananmen Square in Beijing in the first of a series of demonstrations against the Communist government. The protests continued until June 4, when Chinese government troops cracked down.

A Beijing University student argues with policemen in Tiananmen Square, April 27, 1989.

TROOPS ATTACK AND CRUSH BEIJING PROTEST

By Nicholas D. Kristof
Beijing, June 4, 1989

Tens of thousands of Chinese troops retook the center of the capital early this morning from pro-democracy protesters, killing scores of students and workers and wounding hundreds more as they fired submachine guns at crowds of people who tried to resist.

Troops marched along the main roads surrounding central Tiananmen Square, sometimes firing in the air and sometimes firing directly at crowds of men and women who refused to move out of the way. Early this morning, the troops finally cleared the square after first sweeping the area around it. Several thousand students who had remained on the square throughout the shooting left peacefully, still waving the banners of their universities. Several armed personnel carriers ran over their tents and destroyed the encampment.

Reports on the number of dead were sketchy. Three Beijing hospitals reported receiving at least sixty-eight corpses of civilians and said many others had not been picked up from the scene. Four other hospitals said they had received bodies of civilians but declined to disclose how many. Students said, however, that at least five hundred people may have been killed in the crackdown.

Most of the dead had been shot, but some had been run over by armored personnel carriers that forced their way through barricades erected by local residents.

The official news programs this morning reported that the People's Liberation Army had crushed a "counterrevolutionary rebellion" in the capital. They said that more than 1,000 police and troops had been injured and some killed, and that civilians had been killed, but did not give details.

Changan Avenue, or the Avenue of Eternal Peace, Beijing's main east-west thoroughfare, echoed with screams this morning as young people carried the bodies of their friends away from the front lines. The dead or seriously wounded were heaped on the backs of bicycles or tricycle rickshaws and supported by friends who rushed through the crowds, sometimes sobbing as they ran.

The avenue was lit by the glow of several trucks and two armed personnel carriers that students and workers set afire, and bullets swooshed overhead or glanced off buildings. The air crackled almost constantly with gunfire and tear-gas grenades.

It was too early to tell if the crackdown would be followed by arrests of student leaders, intellectuals who have been critical of the party, or members of Zhao's faction. Blacklists have been widely rumored, and many people have been worried about the possibility of arrest.

Students and workers tried to resist the crackdown and destroyed at least sixteen trucks and two armored personnel carriers. Scores of students and workers ran alongside the personnel carriers, hurling concrete blocks and wooden staves into the treads until they ground to a halt. They then threw firebombs at one until it caught fire and set the other alight after first covering it with blankets soaked in gasoline.

The drivers escaped but were beaten by students. A young American man, who could not be immediately identified, was also beaten by the crowd after he tried to intervene and protect one of the drivers.

Many Troops Reported Hurt

Clutching iron pipes and stones, groups of students periodically advanced toward the soldiers. Some threw bricks and firebombs at the lines of soldiers, apparently wounding many of them.

Many of those killed were throwing bricks at the soldiers, but others were simply watching passively or standing at barricades when soldiers fired directly at them.

Two groups of young people commandeered city buses to attack the troops. About ten people were in each bus, and they held firebombs or sticks in their hands as they drove toward lines of armored personnel carriers and troops. Teenage boys, with scarves wrapped around their mouths to protect themselves from tear gas, were behind the steering wheels and gunned the engines as they weaved around the debris to approach the troops.

A lone man confronts a line of tanks in Tiananmen Square on June 6, 1989. He was later pulled away by bystanders and the tanks moved forward.

The first bus was soon stopped by machine-gun fire, and only one person—a young man who jumped out a back window and ran away—was seen getting out. Gunfire also stopped the second bus, and it quickly caught fire, perhaps ignited by the firebomb of someone inside. No one appeared to escape.

Casualty Figures in Doubt

It was also impossible to determine how many civilians had been killed or injured. Beijing Fuxing Hospital, 3.3 miles to the west of Tiananmen Square, reported more than thirty-eight deaths and more than one hundred wounded, and said that many more bodies had yet to be taken to its morgue. A doctor at the Beijing Union Medical College Hospital, two miles northeast of the square, reported seventeen deaths. Beijing Tongren Hospital, one mile southeast of the square, reported thirteen deaths and more than one hundred critically wounded.

"As doctors, we often see deaths," said a doctor at the Tongren Hospital. "But we've never seen such a tragedy like this. Every room in the hospital is covered with blood. We are terribly short of blood, but citizens are lining up outside to give blood."

Four other hospitals also reported receiving bodies but refused to say how many.

In addition, this reporter saw five people killed by gunfire and many more wounded on the east side of the square. Witnesses described at least six more people who had been run over by armored personnel carriers, and about twenty-five more who had been shot to death in the area. It was not known how many bodies remained on the square or how many people had been killed in other parts of the capital.

It was unclear whether the violence would mark the extinction of the seven-week-old democracy movement or would prompt a new phase in the uprising, like a general strike. The violence in the capital ended a period of remarkable restraint by both sides and seemed certain to arouse new bitterness and antagonism among both ordinary people and Communist Party officials for the government of Prime Minister Li Peng.

"Maybe We'll Fail Today"

"Our government is already done with," said a young worker who held a rock in his hand, as he gazed at the army forces across Tiananmen Square. "Nothing can show more clearly that it does not represent the people."

Another young man, an art student, was nearly incoherent with grief and anger as he watched the body of another student being carted away, his head blown away by bullets.

"Maybe we'll fail today," he said. "Maybe we'll fail tomorrow. But someday we'll succeed. It's a historical inevitability."

Recuers help demonstrators wounded in the government's crackdown in Tiananmen Square.

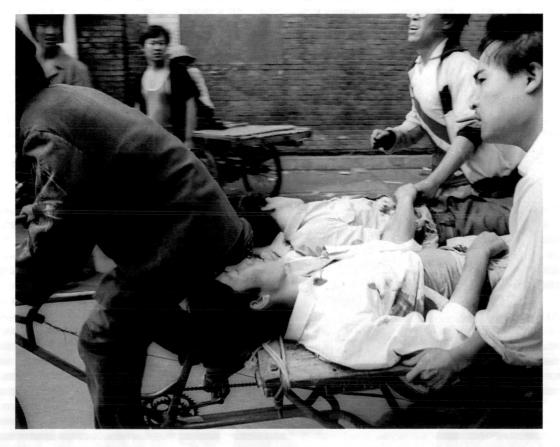

After Hungary loosened restrictions on travel across its border, thousands of East Germans fled. This article from October 1, 1989, captures the arrival in West Germany of several thousand emigrants who had flooded the German embassy in Czechoslovakia, demanding safe passage to the West.

An East German refugee celebrates his departure from Prague on a "freedom train" bound for West Germany.

MORE THAN 6,000 EAST GERMANS SWELL TIDE OF ÉMIGRÉS TO THE WEST

By Serge Schmemann
Hof, West Germany, October 1, 1989

From early this morning, packed East German trains pulled into this border junction town at three-hour intervals, disgorging exhausted East Germans whose departure had been allowed only the day before through an extraordinary face-saving arrangement reportedly approved by Erich Honecker, the East German leader.

By day's end, more than 5,500 East Germans who had taken refuge at the West German embassy in Prague and 800 more from Bonn's embassy in Warsaw arrived at Hof, near the juncture of West Germany's borders with East Germany and Czechoslovakia, after a ten-hour trip that took them back through the country they were leaving.

In Prague, several hundred more East Germans eluded the Czechoslovak police to gain sanctuary at the embassy. It was not clear whether the new arrivals would be covered by the agreement.

Detour Is Center Stage

West German officials said the device that finally enabled East Germany to approve the departure was the detour through East Germany, proposed by Foreign Minister Hans-Dietrich Genscher on Friday. The arrangement enabled East Berlin to contend that the refugees had first come home, as it had repeatedly demanded of them, and on Saturday morning, the Communist government agreed.

The deal also permitted stops in Dresden and Karl-Marx-Stadt, where more émigrés managed to climb aboard the train. According to the refugees, other East Germans gathered to wave as they sped past.

"This was the most moving hour in my political career," said Genscher, who himself fled from East Germany in the

1950s, in describing his trip to Prague Saturday night to tell the East Germans of their impending release. "You can see what people will go through so that they can live like we do—not in the material sense, but to have the right to decide for themselves what to do with their lives."

The developments suggested that the summerlong exodus of East Germans and the occupation of West German embassies were far from over. "Our embassies will not be walled shut," a West German Interior Ministry official, Horst Waffenschmidt, said.

The arrangement to free the East Germans underscored the problem facing both Germanys as the result of the exodus, which began when Hungary dismantled the barbed wire from its border with Austria. More than 30,000 East Germans have fled illegally, most of them crossing from Hungary since September 10, when the Budapest government lifted restrictions on westward travel.

Those who arrived in Hof today were bleary after a sleepless night. For most, there were still hours to go as they waited for transportation to reception camps.

Some had spent weeks at the embassy. Others had made the move at the eleventh hour. Heike Schuberg, a twenty-two-year-old hairdresser from Halle, and her boyfriend, Andreas Stolz, twenty, took the plunge Saturday night on hearing on the radio that the Germans in Prague had been allowed to leave.

Gifts for the Newcomers

Hundreds of Bavarians from Hof and villages scores of miles away crowded the station throughout the day, cheering and waving as the trains pulled in. They built huge mounds of used clothing, toys, baby carriages, and shoes for the newcomers. Some pressed cash into the hands of young parents or handed candy bars to small children.

Others stood silent, burdened with emotions they could not fully explain. For many of the older Germans, the moment seemed to raise difficult memories of a time when they gathered their few belongings after the war and undertook new lives in the West.

Rosa-Marie Olbrich said she visualized herself at eleven, arriving at this same station in 1945. When she heard the news that the trains were coming, she woke up her son, gathered toys and clothes, and came to the station. "I can't find the words to describe what I feel when I see these little children," she said, her eyes moist. "It's like jumping into ice water for them. I know it well."

More Immigrants for Bonn

For West Germany, the flight has meant a flood of new settlers at a time when the country's capacity has already been strained by tens of thousands of ethnic Germans arriving from the Soviet Union and East European countries, as well as an estimated 100,000 East Germans expected to immigrate this year legally.

It is an article of political and constitutional faith in West Germany, however, that all East Germans are fellow Germans, eligible for the benefits and privileges of West German citizenship.

Crowds gathered day and night in Prague's Wenceslas Square to demand democratic reform in Czechoslovakia. On November 24, 1989, the Communist leaders there stepped down, moving another Eastern European nation closer to freedom.

Alexander Dubček, who presided over the Prague spring twenty years earlier, speaks to a crowd of 500,000 Czechoslovaks in Wenceslas Square on November 24, 1989.

IN WENCESLAS SQUARE, A SHOUT: FREEDOM!

By Esther B. Fein

Prague, November 24, 1989

Word surged through the crowd like a current, and it seemed that within seconds every one of the hundreds of thousands of people in Wenceslas Square learned that the entire Czechoslovak Communist Party leadership had resigned.

For nearly a week they had been gathering daily on the cobbled square, waiting to hear those words, and when they did they threw their arms around strangers, colleagues, mothers, lovers, children, and then they all began to shout "Svabodu!"—freedom.

"This is the first time in my life that I have been able to say the word *freedom* and to feel that I am indeed a free man," said Bohumil Stepon, a truck driver from Prague who was crying in the middle of the square. "For forty years, I have lived under the Communist dictatorship. We could not talk freely, we could not think freely, but we became fed up, all of us here. And now, we will never stop saying this word: Freedom! Freedom!"

To the people in Wenceslas Square, the action by the party today was a victory won by the many hours in which they stood in the square affirming their opposition.

The strongest, most persistent reminder to the long-entrenched Czechoslovak leadership that the citizens of this country wanted change came from the hundreds of thousands of ordinary Czechs and Slovaks who appeared at Wenceslas Square in the center of Prague, standing in the chilly air during the days and through much of the nights, calling for freedom.

In the crowd were people who had come daily, leaving work a few hours early, or bundling their children against the crisp cold and bringing them along, or traveling hours from towns miles from the capital.

"Beginning of a Victory"

Most of them wore ribbons that were blue, red, and white, the colors of the official Czechoslovak flag. And they were here again tonight, under a dribbly, raw sky—old people with lined faces, leaning on canes, young students vigorously waving Czechoslovak flags, factory workers with the day's grime still on their hands, and fathers with sons perched on their shoulders, looking down on a quarter mile of human longing that turned into celebration.

A forty-one-year-old technical designer, Rudolf Formanek, came to the rally every day with his seven-year-old son, Jakub, and his thirteen-year-old daughter, Barbara. When he heard the news of the leadership's mass resignation tonight, he pulled them to his chest and told them that this was a day they would remember for the rest of their lives.

"This is the beginning of a victory we once dared to dream of only in our hearts," he said. "We are facing an ecological disaster, a political disaster, and an economic disaster. The books we want to read are not published, artists cannot freely express themselves, and the people's thoughts are imprisoned. Under such conditions, I felt I had to come here, to convince myself that there is a chance for change. And I was right, my God, I was right."

For a while, it seemed as if the highlight of the day would be the arrival of Alexander Dubček, the man who in 1968 presided over the liberal changes of the Prague spring, from Bratislava, where he has been living as a pensioner after retiring from a local forestry department bureau.

Crisis and the Invasion of '68

When he stood on the balcony of the newspaper *Svobodnoye Slovo*, a living symbol of the country's only recent memory of change, people in the square clapped their hands, stomped, and chanted: "Long live Dubček!"

In a speech that echoed from the dozens of speakers hanging on balconies around the square, Dubček told the crowd, "Today's crisis was caused by the invasion of 1968."

"We have been living in darkness for so long," he said. "Even if there was a sign of dawn, that was twenty years ago. But why should we live in the darkness if we know that we can experience the dawn?"

Dubček seemed as stunned and thrilled as many of the demonstrators in Wenceslas Square when he heard the news that the party leadership had stepped down. He was on stage at the Magic Theater, holding a press conference this evening with the playwright Vaclav Hável, a leader of Civic Forum and the human rights group Charter 77, when someone came on stage and whispered in Hável's ear.

Hável leaned over to Dubček and whispered to him. The former leader gasped, then smiled. The beaming men then passed the word on to the journalists in the room, opened a bottle of champagne, and said, "Long live free Czechoslovakia."

Later, when the word reached those in the square, many produced their own bottles. Drivers who heard the news on the car radios passed the square and blew their horns.

While many countries in Eastern Europe made the switch to democracy peacefully, the change of power in Romania was the result of a bloody rebellion. This article from The New York Times, *written shortly after the execution of Romania's dictator, Nicolae Ceausescu, shows the anger that was felt by both Westerners and his own people.*

Civilians crouch behind a tank fighting pro-Ceausescu troops in Bucharest, December 23, 1989.

ROMANIA'S YEARS OF DESPERATION

By Clyde Haberman
Bucharest, Romania, December 31, 1989

To the end, Nicolae Ceausescu was uncompromising. Never mind the tide of reform sweeping other Communist countries, he declared.

Romania would change, in his words, when pears grew on poplar trees. It would, in other words, continue to suffer his special brand of despotism, in which the one commodity not in short supply was fear.

Because he would not bend, Ceausescu had to break. And so the last of the Warsaw Pact dominoes has not just fallen; it has come crashing down in a burst of bloodshed and turmoil not experienced anywhere else in Eastern Europe throughout this year when Communism fell apart.

Thousands of Romanians lay dead last week—shot, bayoneted, or run over with tanks by Ceausescu's security forces. First, the Ceausescu loyalists mowed down antigovernment demonstrators in the northwestern city of Timisoara, where protests on December 17 set off the rush of events that would quickly bring the dictator's downfall. More protests, and deaths, occurred a few days later in Bucharest. Then, even after the president was toppled on December 22, an unknown number of diehards from a crack security unit filled the streets with terror as they fired on innocent people from snipers' nests.

An Unmourned Departure

Among the dead were Ceausescu and his power-driven wife, Elena, who left this world unmourned by their people, in a style alien to postwar Europe. They were summarily tried by a special military tribunal, found guilty of a murderous and larcenous twenty-four-year rule, and put before a firing squad. So many soldiers volunteered for this assignment that their commanders reportedly used a lottery to pick the squad members.

In Bucharest and smaller cities, a sense of menace took hold for a while as streets were deserted and armed bands of civilians, often teenagers, constituted the forces of order.

A provisional government stepped in immediately, one that seemed to have been organized during the death throes of the old regime. Called the Council of the National Salvation Front and led by Ion Iliescu, it is a disparate collection of politicians, poets, and professors who apparently had never sat together as a full group.

Real authority, though, seems to lie in a few hands within this group. And that authority was established right away as the council pledged free elections, warned that terrorists would face the same fate as the Ceausescus unless they laid down their weapons, and scrapped some of Ceausescu's more hated policies. A plan to bulldoze thousands of villages in the name of agricultural efficiency was dropped. So was the thought-control requirement that typewriters be registered with the government.

While some politically minded Romanians objected to the council on the ground that it included too many old Communists, most people seemed ready to give it a chance. Demonstrations were meager. The appetite for street disorder was also small, and general calm returned. There were even questions now about how much carnage had actually occurred in the intense fighting between troops loyal to the new government and the Ceausescu security guards.

Why in Romania?

Why in Romania? At one point last week, some foreign news reports said as many as 80,000 people had been killed nationwide since December 17. But that figure seems implausibly inflated. A Western diplomat said less than 10,000 was more likely; many Romanians and foreigners, asking where all the bodies disappeared to, suspect that the final estimates will be smaller yet.

Nevertheless, the violence was significant and ugly, and an obvious question is why it occurred here and not elsewhere in the Eastern Bloc. An answer probably lies in the special nature of Ceausescu's long rule.

It is hard to understate the nightmarish aspects of his years. To pay off an $11 billion foreign debt at breakneck speed, he insisted that Romania export everything possible, leaving almost nothing behind for his people. Pigs' feet that dangled in otherwise bare butcher shops were jokingly referred to as "patriots" because they were the only part of the animal that stayed home.

But it was not funny. Romanians had little food. They were forced to spend winters in unheated apartments, each lighted by a single bulb. And whether indoors or out, they lived with pervasive fear of the secret police and even of neighbors who might report them.

At Last, Pork and Oranges

After Ceausescu's execution, Romanians had a taste of what they had been missing. Suddenly, for the first time in years, coffee appeared in the stores, along with pork filets and oranges. There also were long lines to get at these rarities. The sad part was that the food had been there all along in this agriculturally productive country; it just had to be liberated from export warehouses.

The possibility of reunification inspired many different reactions across Germany.
Nine different viewpoints were captured in this article in 1990.

A construction site in East Berlin in 1994. Reunification paved the way for dramatic improvements in East German infrastructure.

VOICES OF THE NEW GERMANY

Berlin, October 3, 1990

The feelings of the Germans toward their reunification have always been complex and contradictory.

On the official level, the two Germanys were diametrically opposed in attitude; West Germany enshrined the longing for unity in the Constitution while East Germany considered division permanent and immutable. On the personal level, attitudes among people ranged from open longing to open disdain.

There were those, like Foreign Minister Hans-Dietrich Genscher, who had been compelled to flee the East and lived in the hope of reunification. There were also West Germans, often of an older generation, who harbored feelings of guilt about division, since it had singled out a portion of the nation for prosperity and freedom and a minority for poverty and repression.

In East Germany the yearning for unity was more universal because it figured as a taboo and because the nation was compelled to live with images of the West always on its television screens.

But there were also Germans on both sides who found certain propriety in division. Those ranged from leftists who saw in union the potential for a revival of German nationalism and dangerous ambition to East German intellectuals who dreamed of transforming the Communist dictatorship into a benign, Socialist "third way," free of the commercialism of the West.

But in the end, union came in a way neither the advocates nor the critics expected, and which neither side could avoid. Whether skeptical or jubilant, the majority of Germans were compelled to accept that unification was suddenly a fact. Reactions ranged widely, from open jubilation to deep skepticism. With the merger of the economies of the two Germanys on July 1, an anxiety set in in both Germanys over the realization that unity would cost considerably more than anyone had expected, in mass unemployment in the East and higher taxes in the West.

But it has been clear to anyone in Germany over the last eleven months that for all the grumbling, for all the public expressions of skepticism, there is also a deep satisfaction.

Here are the reactions of nine Germans from varying generations and walks of life. They are not necessarily representative of the nation at large, but they illustrate at least the complexity of a nation's response to its unexpected fortune.

Hans Modrow
"It Comes at the Expense of the Citizens"

A Communist with a reputation as a reformer, he was named transitional prime minister of East Germany in November 1989 and led the country until elections in March 1990.

I wish I could describe October 3 as a historical day without any reservations. Doubtlessly the overcoming of the decades-long division of the German people is of great historic moment, and this not only for the Germans. This day is also of no small importance for the other people, particularly in Europe, as well as for East-West relations generally.

A dangerous hotbed of confrontation, where the mightiest military alliances equipped with sophisticated weapons of mass destruction were facing each other, has been abolished once and for all.

But if I said at the beginning that I am not without reservations, it is because this unification was done in such a way that it comes at the expense of the citizens of the former GDR and, sooner or later, of the people in the Federal Republic of Germany too. The crises in industry and agriculture, soaring unemployment figures, growing social tension, and increasing existential fears in East Germany are only a few consequences of the Kohl and de Maiziere governments' crash course toward unity. A gradual merger of two equal states, for which concrete proposals were submitted during my term as the GDR's prime minister, could have helped to avoid many problems that came up, and still will come up.

Gottfried Forck
"A Lot of Work Remains to Be Done"

Evangelical Protestant Bishop of Berlin-Brandenburg.

A year ago in many towns of the GDR, we assembled for intercession services in churches. We prayed for more justice and freedom. But on October 3,

1989, there was no telling whether our prayers would help us toward these ends. Then, through nonviolent demonstrations, a bloodless revolution began as a result of which the Socialist Unity [Communist] Party had to give up its claim to being the leading party. Christians could interpret this only as a gift of God.

The cracking of the wall, the opening of the borders, free elections, negotiations for the unification of the two German states, the currency union, and now the merger happened in such a rapid succession that we Germans hardly came to our senses. If we had given ourselves more time, many things could have been resolved in a better way. For example, many people in the GDR became jobless as a result of the introduction of the market economy. Moreover, the past under Socialist rule has not been dealt with sufficiently.

Therefore, a lot of work remains to be done.

**UTE LEMPER
"Unification Brings a Lot of Problems"**
A popular singer and actress from West Germany.

There is not a lot to celebrate today because the unification brings a lot of problems with it. Aside from the economic problems the East will have to deal with, there are also very real psychological problems. Those people were educated in a different way for more than forty years. Now they feel guilty that they have themselves believed the wrong things and taught their children the wrong things.

There is also great fear. The fear in the West is mostly about the cost of unification and higher taxes. But in the East they are concerned about not only their livelihood but also being relegated to the status of a third-class country for the next fifteen years.

I have made a number of tours in East Germany this last year. I just returned from Weimar. It is devastating to see. Nothing has been done to maintain the beauty of the cities. The infrastructure has fallen apart.

The people are demonstrating again now, because they are losing their jobs and they are afraid of the future.

But there are positive things, things we could learn from the East. Like their use of language. They try to tell the truth. They are not like our politicians, used to issuing empty phrases or outright lying. We have learned to look behind the words to turn them over and examine the meaning. But in the East they are more sincere, more honest, and it is like a fresh wind.

**HANNS JOACHIM FRIEDRICHS
"A United Germany Does Not Frighten Me"**
Television news anchor.

It's primarily a gut feeling, but I am elated at the thought of no longer living in an artificially divided country. I went to boarding school in what became the Soviet zone soon after my departure and the GDR a few years later—the other

Germany, a sovereign state as the Communists would have it. I am older, and like many of my generation I have been unable to perceive the German Democratic Republic as anything but a piece of Germany, temporarily but thoroughly separated from the rest. The idea of a united Germany does not frighten me. I see no new superpower arising east of the Rhine—smallness in geopolitical terms had its rewards and its charm in the last forty-five years. This, I think, is well remembered by the majority of my countrymen. By and large life has been good to them; much is at stake, they will not want to risk it.

forced to accept things without going through the usual and very necessary parliamentary steps.

Also I fear that the citizens' groups and the Greens in both East and West Germany have been incredibly weakened by this process. The economic power groups, business, and the banks have had their say, and they are determined to make a carbon copy there of what we have here. All our ecological, environmental, and, yes, social concerns are being overwhelmed, and there will be no chance to correct the many mistakes we have made here.

They will just be repeated in the East.

Petra Kelly
"Fear That Germany Will Start to Bully"
A founder of the environmental Green movement.

I come from the town of Gunzburg in Bavaria, the hometown of Dr. Mengele, and watching the procedures leading up to the third of October has aroused fear. Fear that Germany will start to bully or subtly to intimidate its neighbors through economic power and political strength and even militarily, because even with reduced troops it is still a strong army with powerful weapons and even its nuclear options are being held open.

I am also angry. Angry that the incredible speed with which this process has been taking place has overridden all the usual parliamentary procedures. We have been completely overwhelmed and

Michael Friedman
"Both German States Have a Responsibility"
A lawyer specializing in international relations, a member of the Frankfurt Jewish Community and of the directorate of the Central Council of Jews in Germany, and a member of the Frankfurt city parliament.

The feelings that I have as regards the unification of Germany are ambivalent, controversial, and marked by my personal life. The outcries for freedom and democracy from the East, and also from the GDR, have moved me and have made me once again aware of the fact that these values rank among the highest benefits of modern civilization. The fact that the Germans in the GDR have now reached these goals gives reason for joy and shows that, in the final analysis, freedom can never be suppressed.

From the Jewish point of view, but not

only from the Jewish, it must be reminded that both German states have a responsibility with regard to their common past—National Socialism and the Holocaust. In the last decades it was scandalous enough that the GDR, because it posed as an "antifascist state," shrugged off its responsibility.

The mental, personal, and collective grappling with the Holocaust must not be considered obsolete or barred by the statute of limitations, because this conflict became tangible for 16 million Germans only in the 1990's. On the contrary, any kind of change in the GDR as a free state must be related to the confession of the outrages of contemporary GDR citizens.

HELMUT SCHMIDT
"The Great Victory of the Will for Freedom"
Chancellor of West Germany from 1974 to 1982 from the Social Democratic Party. Today he is publisher and regular contributor with the liberal weekly Die Zeit.

On the ninth of November 1989, when the Communists finally had to open the Brandenburg Gate between the two parts of Berlin and when the wall started to crumble, this was the great victory of the will for freedom. Only once in all my life did I have another experience that has affected me in the same deep-going way and which caused the same indescribable joy, namely the reunion with my wife upon coming home from World War II.

The abolition of barbed wire and death strips between the two halves of my people was a cause for enormous joy and of deep gratitude for the vast majority of us Germans. The festivities on the third of October therefore are just an official footnote. But they remind the Germans, so I am convinced, to rest our hopes and our confidence on a persistent continuation of the policies of the Federal Republic of Germany.

MANFRED STOLPE
"Original Enthusiasm Has Dimmed"
Former president of the Consistory of the Protestant Church in Berlin-Brandenburg.

Rarely in history will the passing away of a sovereign state be greeted by so little mourning and such widespread satisfaction and even relief as in the case of the GDR. Only one year ago, the Communist gerontocracy at the helm was toppled by people who courageously claimed the simple truth "We are the people." Twelve months later, however, the original enthusiasm has dimmed considerably. A certain disenchantment about democratic procedures has seized people who by this year's end will have been called upon to vote four times. They were prepared for hardship but the actual balance sheet of four decades of economic mismanagement and social suppression proves to be even more disastrous than expected.

Nevertheless, the tenacity with which people in East Germany pursue their course is impressive and deserves the sympathy and respect of all people who joined their rejoicing a year ago. What these people now really need is visible support and a measure of understanding that takes into account that the abolition of a political setting—as despicable as it may have been—leaves people in a psychological void.

CARL H. HAHN
"An Ultimate End to the Chapter"
Chairman of the management board of Volkswagen.

The unification of the two German states puts an ultimate end to the chapter of horrors of World War II and its consequences. It is to be hoped that this biggest European catastrophe of recent history was the last of its kind. We all are deeply moved these days. Without the political commitment of the United States, the abolition of the division of Germany and Europe would have been impossible—even a free Western Europe would have never come into existence. Without the brave men of Solidarity in Poland, the moral force of the Polish church, and the courage of Gorbachev, such a revolution could not have been brought about without bloodshed.

The pace of changes demonstrates how much despair had accumulated in the people of central and Eastern Europe after decades of Communist dictatorship. Probably, the people on this old continent will never forget October 3, and those in Germany and Berlin will commemorate this day in a spirit of particular gratitude and humility.

In recent years, labor unrest has beset what was formerly East Germany. Here, striking workers in Brandenburg-Havel demonstrate.

Central to the problem of reunification was the question of how to make East Germany economically stable.

A demonstrator in 1998 holds a sign protesting the economic effects of reunification. The sign reads, "Ripped off by Honi (Honecker), then ripped off by Kohl, then ripped off by ????"

As Marriage Nears, Germans in the Wealthy West Fear a Cost in Billions

By Ferdinand Protzman
Bonn, September 23, 1990

For most Germans, the burning questions of unification center on money. From Chancellor Helmut Kohl down to Otto Normalverbraucher—the average German consumer—they are wondering what it will cost, who is going to pay for it, and how.

With formal unification taking place on October 3, exact answers to such questions remain elusive.

There is no question about why the money is needed. With unity, the West takes on full financial responsibility for the East. It will have to pay for government, the civil service administration, the social system, the national health system, the military, and the national debt.

To Rebuild the East

At the same time, Bonn must also provide funds for reconstruction of East Germany's crumbling structure and antiquated industries. Factories, roads, railroads, airports, sea and inland ports, canals and waterways, as well as schools, public buildings, and public housing must all be rebuilt, in many cases from the ground up, if they are to approach Western standards within the five or ten years that many experts project.

In addition, Bonn has committed roughly $10 billion to Moscow to provide housing in the Soviet Union for the Soviet troops being withdrawn from East Germany. And to win Soviet approval for unification, the Kohl administration promised that it would continue to supply the East German goods that the Soviet Union relies on, at a cost of millions more dollars.

Where all this money will come from is a subject of heated debate. Kohl's center-right coalition government is relying heavily on the private sector and insisting that no tax increases will be necessary. To cover the cost of unification, the West German finance minister, Theo Waigel, is allowing the federal budget deficit to swell to levels never seen before, and tapping the nation's capital markets to fill the gap.

The Money Is There

One thing is certain: there is plenty of money. West Germany is one of the richest nations on earth, with a booming, export-powered economy that has grown steadily since Kohl became chancellor in 1982. Its industries are modern and efficient, its private banks are among the most powerful in Europe, and, under the watchful eye of the Bundesbank, the West German central bank, the mark has become the number two currency held in reserve by national banks around the world, after the dollar. West Germans also have the second-highest personal savings rate in the world, trailing only the Japanese.

East Germany is just the opposite. While not destitute, it is in a dizzying economic decline. Government and industry are saddled with debts left by forty years of Communist central planning and corruption.

Economists estimate that of the East's 8,000 industrial companies fewer than a fourth are likely to survive in the free market of a unified Germany.

Like many German officials, Blum has now backed away from earlier predictions of rapid recovery in East Germany, the sort of "new economic miracle" that would rival West Germany's reconstruction after World War II.

No More Miracles

"Miracles are only in fairy tales, and there they happen overnight," Blum said recently in an interview with *Der Spiegel* magazine. "In reality it's going to take rather more time." But in terms of stemming the growth of social problems, time is limited. Unemployment is surging, and it is projected that nearly half of the 8.9 million people in the East German workforce could be out of work by the end of the year. That has raised concern in the West that restless and dispossessed Easterners will begin moving westward in search of jobs and better lives.

Prosperity Equals Tranquility

The prospect of growing uncertainty particularly troubles West Germans, who regard stability, financial security, and prosperity as essential pillars of social order.

In both East and West, there are worries that the unified nation will be less than the sum of its parts. Germans' anxiety is rooted in the memory of earlier periods of economic uncertainty that helped to shape Germany's troubled past.

To ease such concerns, Bonn is eager for foreign companies to become involved in rebuilding East Germany, and as Waigel says, "We have stressed that everything taking place here is happening within a European and international framework."

But even without such intervention the cost of unifying will spread beyond German borders to strain the international financial system. In recent years, West Germany has been a capital exporter, investing the funds gained by exporting in the United States and other European nations. Those flows will drop dramatically, government officials concede.

The conversion of East Germany to the West German currency was the first step in reunification, giving many East Berliners a cause to celebrate.

GERMANS REVEL AS ECONOMIES UNITE

By Serge Schmemann

East Berlin, Sunday, July 1, 1990

At the stroke of midnight, East Germany today formally ceded its currency and economy to West Germany. Thousands of East Germans gathered in the center of the city broke into cheers, firecrackers popped, and car horns blared.

It was not yet formal reunification, but in effect it marked the end of the unsuccessful economic experiment that the former Communist government forcibly imposed on the East German people for forty years, until the regime fell amid the wave of change sweeping Eastern Europe last fall.

As the East German economy came formally under the control of West Germany, the West German mark became the legal tender of both Germanys, all protective tariffs were lifted, and East Germany came under free-market rules.

At a new branch of Deutsche Bank, West Germany's largest commercial bank, on Karl Marx Allee in the heart of East Berlin, several thousand people whooped and pushed forward as the manager opened the doors precisely at midnight to admit the first East Germans. The crush was so great that a plate-glass window shattered and some people fainted.

The bank had announced that it would open at midnight so East Germans could start withdrawing the West German marks they now own instead of East German marks. A bank official sat in a patrol car outside the bank, reassuring the crowd that there was plenty of money to go around.

All around the center throngs of people celebrated with beer and champagne, or simply peered into the display windows of shops newly outfitted by West German companies. The windows of what had been the largest department store in East Berlin, now part of a large West German chain, were decorated with Japanese cameras, French lingerie, and West German bathroom accessories.

One woman said excitedly that it was "such a beautiful feeling" to have the new marks.

A group of West German youths shouted "Happy Birthday!" and tried to sing the forbidden first verse of the West German national anthem, "Deutschland, Deutschland Uber Alles," but nobody remembered the words. One intoxicated man angrily marched off, muttering to a reporter, "Just write down 'This is the end.'"

But for most it was a beginning, a tangible linkup with the prosperous West Germany that the East Germans had spent the last forty years peeking at through television.

Border Formalities End

Simultaneous with the economic merger, all border formalities fell away, and cars flowed through scores of gaps in what had been the Berlin Wall, without slowing down.

A worker disposes of East German marks, made worthless by the switch to West German currency.

1871 First unified German state is formed under Otto Van Bismarck.

1918
Nov. 11: Armistice is signed by Allied and German representatives, bringing an end to World War I.

WORLD WAR I: 1914–18

1910

1914 June 28: Archduke Franz Ferdinand (left), heir to the Austro-Hungarian throne, is assassinated by a Serbian terrorist, sparking a chain of events that leads to World War I.

1917 Nov. 6: "October" revolution establishes a Communist government in Russia (in the Julian Calendar, still in use in Russia, date is Oct. 25, 1917).

1919 Representatives from Allied countries sign the Treaty of Versailles, outlining terms for demilitarization and reparations to be paid by the German government in compensation for World War I.

Archduke Franz Ferdinand (left)

WORLD WAR II: 1939–45

1930

1933 Jan. 30: Adolf Hitler becomes chancellor of Germany.

1939 Sept. 1: Germany invades Poland.

Sept. 3: Britain and France declare war on Germany.

Sept. 27: Warsaw surrenders to Germany after a short but bitter siege, marking the collapse of Polish resistance.

Adolf Hitler

1922 Dec.: Russia, Ukraine, Belarus, and the Transcaucasian states (Georgia, Armenia, and Azerbaijan) unite to form the Union of Soviet Socialist Republics (USSR), commonly known as the Soviet Union. Joseph Stalin becomes general secretary of the Communist Party.

Joseph Stalin

1923 Nov.: German inflation reaches its high point; exchange rate is one trillion German marks to one U.S. dollar.

500-million mark note

1930

1944 June 6: D-Day. The United States and Great Britain launch an offensive from the west, landing in Normandy in northern France.

Aug. 25: Paris is liberated.

Sept. 12: Allied invasion of Germany from the west begins.

1941 April 6: Germany invades Yugoslavia and Greece.

June 22: German army invades Soviet Union.

Dec. 8: United States enters the war.

1946 March 5: Winston Churchill gives "iron curtain" speech in Fulton, Missouri.

1948 June 24: Soviet troops blockade Berlin.

1940 April 9: German troops occupy Denmark and invade Norway.

May 14: Netherlands surrenders to Germany.

May 31: Belgium surrenders to Germany.

June 13: German troops march into Paris.

1942 Aug.: German army reaches Stalingrad.

1943 Feb. 2: Battle of Stalingrad ends in victory for the Soviet Union.

Dec. 7: Roosevelt, Churchill, and Stalin announce an agreement, reached at a conference at Tehran, to work together for the defeat of Germany.

1945 Feb. 8: Allied leaders meet at Yalta.

April 27: American troops, advancing across Germany from the West, meet Soviet troops, advancing from the East, cutting Germany in two.

April 30: Adolf Hitler commits suicide.

May 7: Germany signs an unconditional surrender.

1949 April 4: Twelve European countries form the North Atlantic Treaty Organization (NATO).

May 12: Soviet Union lifts siege of Berlin.

May 23: Zones of Germany occupied by France, England, and the United States combine to form the Federal Republic of Germany (West Germany).

Oct. 7: German Democratic Republic (East Germany) established out of the Soviet occupied zone.

1950

Uprising in Budapest

1954 March 26: East Germany is declared fully sovereign.

1956 Oct. 23: Students protesting for Hungarian autonomy march through Budapest. Soviet tanks and troops quickly intervene. Unable to withstand the might of Soviet forces, students call a cease-fire on November 10, bringing an end to the Hungarian revolt.

1950 Feb. 9: U.S. senator Joseph McCarthy accuses the State Department of employing Communists, and over a period of three years, he conducts a series of public trials accusing Americans of Communist Party affiliation.

June 25: North Korean troops advance across the border into South Korea, sparking the Korean War. The United Nations sends troops to the defense of South Korea—the Soviet Union and China support North Korea. The war ends in a cease-fire on June 27, 1953, with little change to the Korean borders.

1953 March 5: Joseph Stalin dies.

June 17: Soviet troops bring a violent end to massive labor strikes in East Germany.

Sept. 7: Nikita Khrushchev becomes general secretary of the Communist Party in the Soviet Union.

1955 May 5: West Germany is declared fully sovereign.

May 14: Eight Eastern European countries, including the Soviet Union, sign the Warsaw Pact, forming a military alliance designed to counterbalance NATO.

1970

Berlin Wall

1961 East German exodus through West Berlin peaks.

Aug. 17: During the night, East Germany places barbed wire and armed guards across the border between East and West Berlin.

Aug. 24: Günter Litwin becomes the first person to be shot while trying to cross the Berlin Wall.

BERLIN WALL: 1961–89

1963 June 26: Kennedy delivers his "Ich bin ein Berliner" speech from the steps of city hall in West Berlin.

1964 Aug. 7:
The United States Congress approves the Gulf of Tonkin resolution, authorizing a full-scale military intervention in Vietnam, where Soviet-backed North Vietnamese troops have been battling South Vietnamese troops since 1959. The Vietnam War ends in victory for North Vietnam. On July 2, 1976, North and South Vietnam unite to form the Socialist Republic of Vietnam.

John F. Kennedy
"Ich bin ein Berliner."

1962 Aug. 17: East German guards shoot 18-year-old Peter Fechter as he tries to flee across the Berlin Wall. He later dies.

Oct. 14: American spy planes determine that the Soviet Union has placed nuclear missiles in Cuba, making them a potential threat to half of the United States. A crisis follows, in which nuclear war is feared. The situation is resolved by diplomatic means on October 28.

Peter Fechter

1968 Jan. 5: Alexander Dubček is appointed first secretary of the Communist Party in Czechoslovakia, beginning a period of anti-Soviet reform later known as the Prague spring. During the night on August 20, 1968, 200,000 Warsaw Pact troops and 5,000 tanks roll into Prague and bring an end to the reform movement.

1990 May 6: East Germany holds free elections, bringing into office a slate of politicians who have pledged reunification with West Germany.

July 2: East Germans begin to exchange East German marks for West German marks.

July 16: Helmut Kohl meets with Mikhail Gorbachev in Stavropol to negotiate a plan for reunification.

Sept. 12: Soviet Union, United States, Great Britain, and France sign treaty officially ending 45 years of occupation in Germany.

Oct. 3: East and West Germany reunify, becoming one nation with Berlin as its capital.

1985 March 11: Mikhail Gorbachev comes to power in Soviet Union.

1987 June: Ronald Reagan delivers speech at City Hall in Berlin, challenging Gorbachev to "tear down this wall."

1990

Ronald Reagan
"Tear down this wall."

1989 April 15: Protestors gather in Tiananmen Square, Beijing. On June 4, Chinese military forces crack down.

June 4: Polish citizens vote in their first openly contested elections in more than 40 years.

Sept. 10: Hungary opens its border with Austria, sparking mass East German emigration.

Nov. 9: Berlin Wall falls open. Thousands swarm the wall and pour into West Berlin.

Nov. 24: Communist leadership of Czechoslovakia steps down.

Dec. 16: Fighting erupts in Timisoara, Romania. The conflict continues until December 25, when dictator Nicolae Ceausescu and his wife are executed.

Source Notes

The following articles from *The New York Times* appear as excerpts, supplemental text, or illustrations:

page 15, 78: Schmemann, Serge. "East Germany Opens Frontier to the West." *The New York Times,* November 10, 1989.

page 72: Schmemann, Serge. "The Soviet State, Born of a Dream, Dies." *The New York Times,* December 26, 1991.

page 76: Schmemann, Serge. "Rallying Cry of East Berliners: Gorbachev!" *The New York Times,* June 10, 1987.

page 80: Maps and captions were drawn from two articles:

"Shifting Borders: Conquest, Defeat, and Division." *The New York Times,* November 12, 1989.

Bernstein, Richard. "Several Germanys Since 1871, But Today's is 'Very Different.'" *The New York Times,* October 3, 1990.

page 82: DeParle, Jason. "The Bitter Legacy of Yalta: Four Decades of What-Ifs." *The New York Times,* November 26, 1989.

page 84: Sullivan, Walter. "The 'Sovereignty' of East Germany." *The New York Times,* December 11, 1955.

page 86: "Berliners Gather at Barricade Dividing Families and Friends." *The New York Times,* August 23, 1961.

page 88: Gilroy, Harry. "German Reds Shoot Fleeing Youth, Let Him Die at Wall." *The New York Times,* August 17, 1962.

page 90: Kristof, Nicholas D. "Troops Attack and Crush Beijing Protest; Thousands Fight Back, Scores Are Killed." *The New York Times,* June 4, 1989.

page 94: Schmemann, Serge. "More Than 6,000 East Germans Swell Tide of Émigrés to the West." *The New York Times,* October 2, 1989.

page 96: Fein, Esther B. "In Wenceslas Square, a Shout: Freedom!" *The New York Times,* November 25, 1989.

page 98: Haberman, Clyde. "Rumania's Years of Desperation, Days of Relief." *The New York Times,* December 31, 1989.

page 100: "Voices of the New Germany: Hope, Guilt, Fear, Joy and Deep Satisfaction… In the Words of the Prominent, Glimpses of a Nation's Complex Feelings." *The New York Times,* October 4, 1990.

page 106: Protzman, Ferdinand. "As Marriage Nears, Germans in the Wealthy West Fear a Cost in Billions." *The New York Times,* September 24, 1990.

page 108: Schmemann, Serge. "Germans Revel as Economies Unite." *The New York Times,* July 1, 1990.

Further Reading

Many articles from the archives of *The New York Times* were used in the research for this book. Some of these articles provided valuable insight into the topics covered, but it was impossible to include all of them in these pages. If you wish to dig deeper into some of the events covered, you may enjoy reading the following articles:

The Berlin Wall
"Berlin Wall 7 Years Later; A Grim and Effective Barrier."
The New York Times,
August 12, 1968.

Berkow, Ira. "Joe Namath, Joe Louis and the Berlin Wall."
The New York Times,
November 12, 1989.

Lackenbach, Robert. "The Daily Drama at Checkpoint Charlie."
The New York Times,
March 18, 1962.

McFadden, Robert D. "The Berlin Wall: A Monument to the Cold War, Triumphs and Tragedies."
The New York Times,
November 10, 1989.

Schmemann, Serge. "In Search of a Work of Art to Overcome the Wall."
The New York Times,
November 13, 1987.

Schmemann, Serge. "Legacies by the Wall: Rabbits and Graffiti Bits."
The New York Times,
November 24, 1989.

Changing sovereignty of Germany
"German East Zone Gets 'Sovereignty' but Russians Stay."
The New York Times,
March 26, 1954.

Reuters. "An Outline of German History."
The New York Times,
November 29, 1989.

Construction of the Berlin Wall
"Berliners Live with Reality of Communists' Wall in City."
The New York Times,
June 27, 1963.

"Seek to Prevent More Break-Throughs by Refugees—Communist Railway Policeman Flees and Asks Asylum."
The New York Times,
September 17, 1961.

"Street with Back Door to West Finds Its Escape Nailed Shut."
The New York Times,
August 21, 1961.

Binder, David. "Guards in Berlin Chat across Line."
The New York Times,
November 11, 1961.

Coup against Gorbachev / the end of the Soviet Union
Bohlen, Celestine. "Coup Sets Yeltsin at Center Stage."
The New York Times,
August 20, 1991.

Clines, Francis X. "Communist Flag is Removed; Yeltsin Gets Nuclear Controls."
The New York Times,
December 26, 1991.

Death of Peter Fechter
"300 East Berliners at Funeral of Youth Shot by Guard at Wall."
The New York Times,
August 25, 1962.

"Exchange of Berlin Notes."
The New York Times,
August 28, 1962.

"Statements by Commandants in Berlin."
The New York Times,
August 22, 1962.

Associated Press. "Thousands in Berlin Honor Youth Left to Die at Wall."
The New York Times,
August 18, 1963.

Erich Honecker
Saxon, Wolfgang.
"Erich Honecker, Ruler of East
Germany for 18 of Its Last
Years, Dies in Exile at 81."
The New York Times,
May 30, 1994.

Escapes across the wall
"G.I. Aids Wounded
East German over Wall
amid Gunfire."
The New York Times,
September 14, 1964.

"Youth is Ousted
by East Germany."
The New York Times,
July 22, 1973.

The Associated Press.
"Two Seized in Ruse
by East Germans."
The New York Times,
October 9, 1961.

Lentz, Ellen.
"Two East Germans
Tell of Fleeing."
The New York Times,
October 29, 1972.

Markham, James M.
"Germanys Trafficking
in People."
The New York Times,
July 29, 1989.

Protzman, Ferdinand.
"As East German Émigrés
Take Root in the West,
Their Prosperity Unfurls."
The New York Times,
September 25, 1990.

UPI. "Refugees Need
Luck and Nerve to Breach
Red Wall of Berlin."
The New York Times,
October 7, 1961.

Wilcke, Gerd.
"Bonn Warns Germans."
The New York Times,
August 21, 1962.

Fall of the Berlin Wall
"Berlin Border Guards
Stunned by the News."
The New York Times,
November 10, 1989.

Pear, Robert. "Allies Retain
Authority over West Berlin."
The New York Times,
November 11, 1989.

Protzman, Ferdinand.
"East Berliners Explore
a Land Long Forbidden."
The New York Times,
November 10, 1989.

Protzman, Ferdinand.
"Family Says of the West,
'It's a Dream.'"
The New York Times,
November 12, 1989.

Riding, Alan. "Hoping for
Fall of Less Known Barrier."
The New York Times,
November 14, 1989.

Schmemann, Serge.
"Cheers in the East as
Brandenburg Gate Reopens."
The New York Times,
December 23, 1989.

Whitney, Craig R.
"A City Where Everyone
Is Away for the Holiday."
The New York Times,
November 12, 1989.

Schmemann, Serge.
"For All, East and West,
A Day Like No Other."
The New York Times,
November 12, 1989.

Schmemann, Serge.
"How the Wall Was Cracked—
a Special Report."
The New York Times,
November 19, 1989.

Schmemann, Serge. "The Border
Is Open; Joyous East Germans
Pour Through Wall."
The New York Times,
November 11, 1989.

Fall of the Eastern Bloc
"Before Our Eyes,
the Bloc Splinters."
The New York Times,
August 25, 1989.

Clines, Francis X.
"Ukrainian Voters Crowd
the Polls to Create Nation."
The New York Times,
December 2, 1991.

Passell, Peter. "Unsnarling
a Tangled Trade Alliance."
The New York Times,
January 10, 1990.

Germany in WWII
"Chronology: Highlights of
the Four War Years in Europe."
The New York Times,
June 11, 1944.

"A Chronology of the War in Europe: 100 Outstanding Dates."
The New York Times,
May 6, 1945.

"German Army Attacks Poland."
The New York Times,
September 1, 1939.

"The War in Europe Is Ended; Surrender Is Unconditional."
The New York Times,
May 8, 1945.

**John F. Kennedy's
visit to Berlin**
"Text of Kennedy Statements in Berlin."
The New York Times,
June 27, 1963.

"The President in Berlin."
The New York Times,
June 27, 1963.

Olsen, Arthur.
"President Hailed by over a Million in Visit to Berlin."
The New York Times,
June 27, 1963.

Life in the Communist East
"German Reds Jail Two U.S. Students."
The New York Times,
September 27, 1961.

Baldwin, Hanson W. "To Berlin—High Road and Low."
The New York Times,
October 29, 1961.

Frankel, Max. "You Can't Go Home to Weissenfels."
The New York Times,
January 10, 1965.

Middleton, Drew.
"Policy of 'Liberation' Tough One to Execute."
The New York Times,
March 1, 1953.

Taubman, Philip. "The Perils of Reporting From Moscow."
The New York Times,
September 26, 1986.

**Mikhail Gorbachev
and glasnost**
"Gorbachev's Six Tumultuous Years at Soviet Helm."
The New York Times,
December 16, 1991.

"A Leader with Style— and Impatience."
The New York Times,
March 12, 1985.

"Reform Redux in Russia."
The New York Times,
June 13, 1987.

Schmemann, Serge.
"The Emergence Of Gorbachev."
The New York Times,
March 3, 1985.

Schmemann, Serge.
"Greater 'Glasnost' Turns Some Soviet Heads."
The New York Times,
November 9, 1986.

Schmemann, Serge.
"Two Germanys' Political Divide is Being Blurred by Glasnost."
The New York Times,
December 18, 1988.

Reunification of Germany
Binder, David.
"At Plant in East Berlin, Men Are of Two Minds."
The New York Times,
December 20, 1989.

Binder, David.
"City of Past and Future, Berlin Reunifies Itself."
The New York Times,
August 20, 1990.

Friedman, Thomas L.
"Four Allies Give Up Rights in Germany."
The New York Times,
September 13, 1990.

Kamm, Henry.
"A Foreboding That Unity Means New Risks for Them."
The New York Times,
September 26, 1990.

Page, Eric. "Cold War Sealed Germany's Division."
The New York Times,
November 14, 1989.

Protzman, Ferdinand.
"Westward Tide of East Germans Is a Popular No-Confidence Vote."
The New York Times,
August 22, 1989.

Schmemann, Serge.
"A German Divide Fades, but 2 Towns Still Feel It."
The New York Times,
September 23, 1990.

Schmemann, Serge.
"On Unity's Eve, Subdued Mood
Replaces Euphoria."
The New York Times,
September 30, 1990.

Tagliabue, John.
"New Germany or Not, in the
East It's Same Old Teachers."
The New York Times,
September 29, 1990.

Tagliabue, John. "On New
Era's Eve, Berlin Rejoices."
The New York Times,
October 3, 1990.

Whitney, Craig R.
"From Germany's Neighbors,
Respect and Then Acceptance."
The New York Times,
September 29, 1990.

Whitney, Craig R.
"Severed German Families,
Starting Now to Mend."
The New York Times,
October 1, 1990.

**Ronald Reagan's
visit to Berlin**
"Excerpts from Reagan's
Talk at the Berlin Wall."
The New York Times,
June 13, 1987.

Schmemann, Serge. "24,000
Demonstrate in Berlin Against
Reagan's Visit Today."
The New York Times,
June 12, 1987.

Tiananmen Square
Kristof, Nicholas D.
"China Erupts…
the Reasons Why."
The New York Times,
June 4, 1989.

Uprising in Romania
"Two American and Two
European Journalists Shot
and Wounded."
The New York Times,
December 25, 1989.

Kifner, John.
"Bucharest Tension."
The New York Times,
December 25, 1989.

Fischer, Mary Ellen.
"Rumania: Up For Grabs."
The New York Times,
December 28, 1989.

Tagliabue, John.
"December 23, 1989."
The New York Times,
June 15, 1997.

Wave of emigration in 1989
Markham, James M.
"East Germany
Assails Émigrés."
The New York Times,
March 9, 1989.

Schmemann, Serge.
"East Germans Declare Amnesty
for Those Who Fled."
The New York Times,
October 28, 1989.

Schmemann, Serge.
"Hungary Allows 7,000 East
Germans to Emigrate West."
The New York Times,
September 11, 1989.

**Winston Churchill's
"iron curtain" speech**
"Mr. Churchill's Address
Calling for United Effort
for World Peace."
The New York Times,
March 6, 1946.

The Yalta conference
"Text of Big Three
Announcement on the
Crimea Conference."
The New York Times,
February 13, 1945.

Baldwin, Hanson W.
"Agreements at Yalta
Speed Germany's Fall."
The New York Times,
February 18, 1945.

Acknowledgments

Covering a story like the fall of the Berlin Wall and the end of Communism involves many people working many long hours over many weeks and months. I can never thank them all. But I would like to single out Victor Homola, my assistant in East Germany, who was among the first to rush through the wall, and Tom Seibert, my assistant in West Germany, who was brilliant, tireless, and a wonderful companion on countless trips. I also owe a considerable debt of thanks to Bernard Gwertzman, the *New York Times* foreign editor at the time, who managed one of the finest teams of reporters ever assembled with enthusiasm, wisdom, and bottomless patience, and Max Frankel, the executive editor, who followed the story as only someone who had fled Germany as a child could. In this project, I am grateful to Deirdre Langeland of Kingfisher Publications, for her patient and expert editing, and to Alex Ward, the book editor of *The New York Times*, for his insight and support.

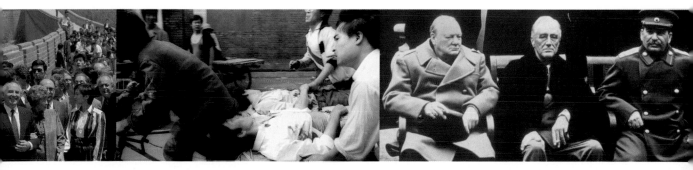

Picture Credits

The publisher would like to thank the following for permission to reproduce their material. Every care has been taken to trace copyright holders. However, if there have been unintentional omissions or failure to trace copyright holders, we apologize and will, if informed, endeavor to make corrections in any future edition.

Key: *b* = bottom, *c* = center, *l* = left, *r* = right, *t* = top, *bg* = background

Cover: AP Wide World

pages 1 *(l to r)*: Peter Turnley/Corbis, Regis Bossu/Corbis Sygma, Stephen Ferry/Getty Images; 2–3 *(l to r)*: Thierry Orban/Corbis Sygma, Dave Houser/Corbis, John Gaps III/AP Wide World, Thierry Orban/Corbis Sygma; 4–5 *(l to r)* Getty Images/Time & LIFE, Patrick Herzog/AFP/Getty Images, AP Wide World, Peter Turnley/ Corbis; 6–7 *(l to r)* Bettmann/Corbis, David Turnley/Corbis, Getty Images/Time & LIFE, Bettmann/Corbis, Peter Turnley/Corbis; 8–9 *(l to r)*: Bernard Bisson/Corbis Sygma, Ralph Crane/Getty Images/Time & LIFE, Peter Turnley/Corbis, Bettmann/Corbis; 13: Wolfgang Kaehler/Corbis *(t)*, Roy Smith/Cordaiy Photo Library Ltd./Corbis; 14: Katherine Young/Poly-Presse; 17: Stapleton Collection/Corbis; 19: Archivo Iconografico SA/Corbis; 20: Pvt.Miller/Corbis *(l)*, Bettmann/Corbis *(c)*; 21: Corbis; 22: Bettmann/Corbis; 23: Yevgeny Khaldei/Corbis; 24: *The New York Times;* 25: BLACK STAR, Thierry Orban/Corbis Sygma; 27: Bettmann/Corbis; 30: AP Wide World *(l, c)*, Bettmann/Corbis; 32: Bettmann/Corbis *(t)*, Getty Images/Time & LIFE-Chris Niedenthal *(bl)*, Owen Franken/Corbis; 35: Bettmann/Corbis *(t)*, Pieter Liebing/AP Wide World; 37: Getty Images/Time & Life; 38: Getty Images/Time & Life; 41: Peter Turnley/Corbis, 42: Peter Turnley/Corbis; 43: Leszek Wdowinski/Reuters/Corbis; 44: Peter Turnley/Corbis *(tl)*, David Turnley/Corbis; 47: Alain Nogues/Corbis Sygma; 48: Thierry Orban/Corbis Sygma; 49: Peter Turnley/Corbis; 51: Camera Press (UK); 52: David Turnley/Corbis; 54: Regis Bossu/Corbis Sygma; 55: David Turnley *(tl, r)*, Peter Turnley/Corbis; 56: Robert Maass/Corbis; 59: Leif Skoogfors/Corbis *(tl)*, Corbis *(tr)*, Bernard

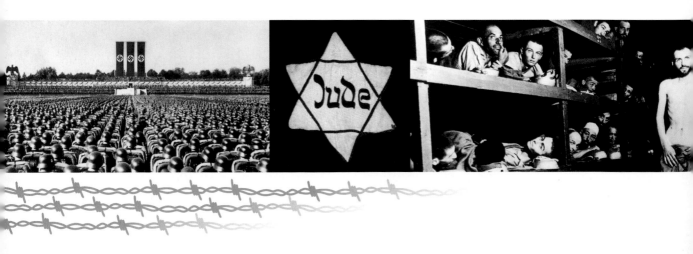

Index